DR. O. WAYNE AND PAMELA R. BREWER

Praying
The *Breath* of life

A STUDY ON
PRAYER
FOR DISCIPLES

ADULT DISCIPLESHIP PUBLISHERS
CLEVELAND, TENNESSEE

Published by Adult Discipleship.

All scripture quotations, unless otherwise indicated, are taken from the Holy Bible, King James Version "KJV" (Public Domain).

Scripture marked NKJV taken from the New King James Version®. Copyright © 1982 by Thomas Nelson, Inc. Used by permission. All rights reserved.

Scripture quotations marked KJ21 are taken from the 21st Century King James Version®, copyright © 1994. Used by permission of Deuel Enterprises, Inc., Gary, SD 57237. All rights reserved.

ISBN: 978-1-940682-08-2
Copyright © 2013 by Adult Discipleship
All Rights Reserved
Printed in the United States of America

DEDICATION

Praying, The Breath of Life is dedicated to our Lord Jesus who is still teaching us how to pray. We further dedicate this volume to our parents, Oliver and Peggy Brewer who continue to live the life of unceasing prayer; and to James and Evelyn Coker who shared with Pam how God miraculously delivered her from death when she was just a toddler. We also dedicate this work to all of the countless family, friends, and other church members who have interceded for us over the years. What a great reward is laid up for you!

TABLE OF CONTENTS

APPENDICES

FOREWORD

One wonders how many early mornings the disciples of Jesus may have awakened around the smoking embers of a still-warm campfire, only to realize that the Master was no longer resting but was kneeling many yards away under the cover of some olive trees, praying to His Father in Heaven. Over time this custom of Jesus came as no surprise to these ever-learning Hebrews. They quickly realized that for their Teacher, this was a discipline—no, much more than a discipline! This praying of Jesus to the Father was His very breath of life. It was as natural and needful for Him as breathing was for the twelve of them. This most essential part of Jesus' earthly ministry impacted and intrigued them to the point that they hungered to participate in this spiritual breath of life. Their desire is recorded in Luke 11.

> And it came to pass, that, as he was praying in a certain place, when he ceased, one of his disciples said unto him, Lord, teach us to pray . . . (v. 1).

Jesus' breath of life was a foretaste to the disciples of what was soon to come after Christ's resurrection on the Day of Pentecost. In the second chapter of Acts, Luke begins to tell the actual account of another breath of life associated with the third person of our triune God.

> And when the day of Pentecost was fully come, they were all with one accord in one place. And

suddenly there came a sound from heaven as of a rushing mighty *wind*, and it filled all the house where they were sitting. And there appeared unto them cloven tongues like as of a fire, and it sat upon each of them. And they were all filled with the Holy Ghost, and began to speak with other tongues, as the Spirit gave them utterance (Acts 2:1-4 italics added).

Rushing wind indeed! This was the Holy Spirit's very breath of life upon a newly born living thing, later to be called the church.

God's church across the world was born in a Jerusalem upper room by the life-giving, corporate prayer of about 120 faith-filled, unified disciples. Spirit-filled believers understand that this very wind (power, influence, anointing) of the Holy Spirit is also the literal inspiration of powerful praying itself. For the disciples of Christ, *praying is the breath of life*.

1 Thessalonians 5:17 tells believers to "Pray without ceasing." Our physical life depends on ceaseless breathing; likewise, our spiritual life depends on unceasing prayer. Praying is life-giving and never truly ends.

Praying, The Breath of Life is not intended to be an encyclopedic source book about prayer, nor a comprehensive catalog of all types, principles, and personalities related to prayer in the Bible. Such an effort could easily be a multi-volume work. Rather, this study on prayer is intended for those who desire to be disciples of Jesus Christ. This work is a topically arranged treatment of various key biblical principles of powerful, effective praying. We have chosen to utilize a number of noteworthy biblical characters as human lessons by which we will note and exemplify spiritually significant characteristics of life-giving prayer. In a word, this biblical treatment is sufficiently in-depth without being complex. It is occasionally exegetical. Some terms from the original New Testament Greek are transliterated and you will find a number of references to the original biblical languages to be keyed to *Strong's Concordance*. In true Pentecostal fashion this book is also a record of testimonies to the glory of God. These come to us straight from the Word, and from more recent prayer experiences in which He has shown His faithfulness and glory. After all, we overcome by the word of our testimony!

It is our conviction that prayer is the breath of life because prayer is intrinsically the substance of our relationship with our Lord. To a great degree, your relationship with God is equal to your prayer life! It is our sincere desire that you will become an evermore perfected, victorious, Christ-like disciple as you discover and put to personal use these biblically-based, time-proven principles of powerful praying. If you are not already convinced that prayer will dramatically change your life, we trust that as you study the lives, struggles, and triumphs of these saints of Scripture, you will become convinced of the irrefutable truth that for all disciples of Jesus Christ, praying truly is the breath of life!

A Special Word of Thanks

A project like this does not come together with the work of only one person. We want to acknowledge those that have been used of the Lord to bring this book into reality.

We wish to thank Joel Barnes and Kristina Higgins for their tireless efforts in editing and editorial suggestions.

Annette Alsobrooks from Ballew Graphics for book cover design.

David and Lorna Gosnell for believing in the project to see it to completion and for publishing, *Praying, The Breath of Life* through Adult Discipleship.

Dr. O. Wayne and Pamela R. Brewer

Praying

Is *Intimacy* with God

DR. O. WAYNE BREWER

Praying, The *Breath* of Life

Scriptures

Genesis 3:8-10

And they heard the voice of the Lord God walking in the garden in the cool of the day: and Adam and his wife hid themselves from the presence of the Lord God amongst the trees of the garden.

And the Lord God called unto Adam, and said unto him, Where art thou?

And he said, I heard thy voice in the garden, and I was afraid, because I was naked; and I hid myself.

Nehemiah 13:7-12

And I came to Jerusalem, and understood of the evil that Eliashib did for Tobiah, in preparing him a chamber in the courts of the house of God.

And it grieved me sore: therefore I cast forth all the household stuff to Tobiah out of the chamber.

Then I commanded, and they cleansed the chambers: and thither brought I again the vessels of the house of God, with the meat offering and the frankincense.

And I perceived that the portions of the Levites had not been given them: for the Levites and the singers, that did the work, were fled every one to his field.

Then contended I with the rulers, and said, Why is the house of God forsaken? And I gathered them together, and set them in their place.

Then brought all Judah the tithe of the corn and the new wine and the oil unto the treasuries.

Psalm 51:1-12, NKJV
Have mercy upon me, O God, According to Your lovingkindness; According to the multitude of Your tender mercies, Blot out my transgressions.

Wash me throughly from mine iniquity, and cleanse me from my sin.

For I acknowledge my transgressions, And my sin is always before me.

Against You, You only, have I sinned, And done this evil in Your sight—That You may be found just when You speak, And blameless when You judge.

Behold, I was brought forth in iniquity, And in sin my mother conceived me.

Behold, You desire truth in the inward parts, And in the hidden part You will make me to know wisdom.

Purge me with hyssop, and I shall be clean; Wash me, and I shall be whiter than snow.

Make me hear joy and gladness, That the bones You have broken may rejoice.

Hide Your face from my sins, And blot out all my iniquities.

Create in me a clean heart, O God, And renew a steadfast spirit within me.

Do not cast me away from Your presence, And do not take Your Holy Spirit from me.

Restore to me the joy of Your salvation, And uphold me by Your generous Spirit.

Psalm 84:1-12
How amiable are thy tabernacles, O Lord of hosts!

My soul longeth, yea, even fainteth for the courts of the Lord: my heart and my flesh crieth out for the living God.

Yea, the sparrow hath found an house, and the swallow a nest for herself, where she may lay her young, even thine altars, O Lord of hosts, my King, and my God.

Blessed are they that dwell in thy house: they will be still praising thee. Selah.

Blessed is the man whose strength is in thee; in whose heart are the ways of them.

Who passing through the valley of Baca make it a well; the rain also filleth the pools.
They go from strength to strength, every one of them in Zion appeareth before God.

O Lord God of hosts, hear my prayer: give ear, O God of Jacob. Selah.

Behold, O God our shield, and look upon the face of thine anointed.

For a day in thy courts is better than a thousand. I had rather be a doorkeeper in the house of my God, than to dwell in the tents of wickedness.

For the Lord God is a sun and shield: the Lord will give grace and glory: no good thing will he withhold from them that walk uprightly.

O Lord of hosts, blessed is the man that trusteth in thee.

Psalm 141:2
Let my prayer be set forth before thee as incense; and the lifting up of my hands as the evening sacrifice.

Matthew 21:12-14
And Jesus went into the temple of God, and cast out all them that sold and bought in the temple, and overthrew the tables of the moneychangers, and the seats of them that sold doves,

And said unto them, It is written, My house shall be called the house of prayer; but ye have made it a den of thieves.

And the blind and the lame came to him in the temple; and he healed them.

Mark 12:30
And thou shalt love the Lord thy God with all thy heart, and with all thy soul, and with all thy mind, and with all thy strength: this is the first commandment.

Praying, The *Breath* of Life

Study

THE REASON THIS BOOK IS ENTITLED *Praying, The Breath of Life* instead of Prayer, The Breath of Life is because true Pentecostal praying is an active, living thing. True praying is not a noun. For disciples of Jesus Christ, prayer is a verb! Let Hindus and Buddhists say a prayer if they insist, but Christians serve a living God to whom we actively, joyfully, and continually pray. Prayer is our breath of life.

Prayer's Highest Priority: Knowing God

The greatest priority of humankind is to love God and enjoy Him in this world and in the world to come. Indeed, God created humanity for the very purpose of fellowshipping with each one intimately in a personal relationship. Praying is a marvelous gift from God whereby we are privileged to actually, personally carry on a relationship with the Creator, who is also our Father. So often people think of God as a means to their own purpose. This is a blatant and tragic misunderstanding. God is not a means to an end. God is the end and praying is the means by which we relate to Him at the deepest levels of our being.

When we learn to call God by His Names in prayer, we will experience an ever growing intimacy with Him. Do we realize that God is: Jehovah Shalom (the Lord is peace), Jehovah Sabaoth (the Lord of hosts), Jehovah Rapha (the Lord Who heals), Jehovah Jireh (the Lord will provide) and Jehovah Tsidqenu (the Lord our righteousness)? These are just a few of His Names which demonstrate the facets of our Father's wonderful, loving nature. Appendix Six has more to say about God's Names. Use His Names when you pray.

Falling Out of Relationship with God

Before their fall into sin in the Garden of Eden, Adam and Eve enjoyed an intimate, fully satisfying relationship with the Lord God. Genesis 3:8 speaks of Adam and Eve hearing "the voice of the Lord God walking in the garden in the cool of the day. . ." It appears that God, in human form (the pre-incarnate Christ) walked and talked with the first couple. Picture it, strolling with God in the cool hours with Him calling you by your name. This is a picture of tranquil intimacy. The phrase "cool of the day" in Hebrew reads "in the wind of the day." Isn't it interesting that thousands of years later, the Holy Spirit would announce His arrival to about 120 praying disciples with another wind—a mighty, rushing wind?

The Genesis narrative continues (vv. 7-8) and tells us that the couple hid themselves from God because they had sinned and become aware of their own nakedness and shame. Then in verse 9, we hear our loving, relationship-seeking God almost painfully calling out to Adam and asking, "Where art thou?" This is where sin entered into the human race and broke the intimacy between God and man, initiating the need of a Savior for us all.

This same story has been repeated an untold number of times as our Lord continues to ask us, "Where are you?" Jesus Christ and Jesus Christ alone is the cure for alienated men and woman who are out of harmony with the living God. However, Jesus cannot save and cleanse our souls unless we repent of our sin.

Restoring Relationship with God

Prayer has many facets, not the least of which is the prayer of confession. We must be truthful with God about our transgressions, for an intimate relationship always demands truth. 1 John 1:9 assures us,

> If we confess our sins, he is faithful and just to forgive us our sins, and to cleanse us from all unrighteousness.

Prayer that gives the gift of intimacy with God refuses to shy away from honest confession of sin and repentance of all that impedes our deepest love for Him. In Psalm 51 (written by David after he was confronted about his terrible sin with Bathsheba), David acknowledged his sin (v. 3), begged for complete cleansing (v. 2), and then got to his deepest concern when he said, "Cast me not away from thy presence; and take not thy holy spirit from me" (v. 11). In other words, David genuinely longed for the return of the close relationship he had previously enjoyed with his God!

Through praying, we demonstrate our yearning for His Presence. Through disobedience and self-will we sacrifice that peace-giving sense of closeness with the Father, only later to realize that nothing in this life is more precious than our intimacy with the Almighty.

The Sweetness of Intimacy with God

Our relationship with God is our greatest treasure. He wants us to want Him. Our prayer life is our special time to touch God and be touched by Him. Like any loving parent, our Father in Heaven enjoys our talking to Him. Psalm 141:2 says, "Let my prayer be set forth before thee as incense; and the lifting up of my hands as the evening sacrifice." The Psalmist says, "How amiable are thy tabernacles, O Lord of hosts!" (Psalm 84:1). To enter His tabernacle is to enter into His presence.

When we pray, we are literally encountering God; encountering God is no small thing. Ask Moses about encountering the presence of God at the burning bush, or Jacob when wrestling with God, or Thomas when he felt the nail-scarred hands of Jesus.

I well remember fervently seeking God for guidance on a very important decision, only to have God's presence fill the upstairs bedroom in which I was praying. His presence was so real, so palpable, that for about 45 minutes I could not raise my head from the carpeted floor in which my face was buried. God was in the room, and all I could do was kneel facedown, weeping, and never daring to lift my face. This is what a broken, submitted child of God does when Divinity moves into a sanctified time and place of prayer.

There is no amount of money that can purchase an audience with the King of Kings—and if there isn't, what can? Simple. Psalm 51:17 declares, "The sacrifices of God are a broken spirit: a broken contrite heart, O God, thou wilt not despise." You see, our Lord wants us to want Him like a thirsty man desires cold water or a hungry man famishes for delicious food. An intimate relationship with God is sweet and sincere. In Psalm 84:2, the writer passionately declares, "My soul longeth, yea, even fainteth for the courts of the Lord: my heart and my flesh crieth out for the living God."

Throwing Out the Thieves

There is an old saying that goes "nobody likes a thief." Have you ever stopped to think that anything that steals prayer from your heart and life is a thief?

Every Church and Every Heart a House of Prayer

In Matthew 21:12-14 is told a fascinating account of Jesus, in a decidedly angry spirit, driving the moneychangers from the temple of God. This incident gives the modern disciple an insight into just how important and holy our hearts and churches are supposed to be. It further teaches us that prayer is to be the preeminent activity in both!

Let's read the account in Matthew 21:

And Jesus went into the temple of God, and cast out all them that sold and bought in the temple, and overthrew the tables of the moneychangers, and the seats of them that sold doves, And said unto them, It is written, My house shall be called the house of prayer; but ye have made it a den of thieves. And the blind and the lame came to him in the temple; and he healed them (vv. 12-14).

Did you notice that, in Jesus' judgment, everything and everybody that was not supposed to be in the temple of God but was there, He called a thief? Are there thieves in the house of the Lord that are taking the place of genuine prayer? Are there thieves in your life that are stealing away your own prayer life? Just like a church sanctuary or a consecrated prayer room, the human (spiritual) heart was intended by the Lord to be the very temple of God, a house of prayer! 1 Corinthians 3:16 asks the question, "Know ye not that ye are the temple of God, and that the Spirit of God dwelleth in you?" 2 Corinthians 6:16 declares outright, ". . . for ye are the temple of the living God . . ." Jesus said in Matthew 21:13, ". . . My house shall be called the house of prayer; but ye have made it a den of thieves."

There comes a time when every local church, every altar, and every Christian's heart needs a cleansing to take place. There comes a time when old spiritual garbage needs to be taken out. There comes a time when the House of Prayer (our heart) needs a housecleaning. The Lord intended His church and our hearts to be places of prayer!

Three Questions About My Heart (God's Temple of Prayer)

Every disciple needs to answer three crucial questions about their own heart (temple/house of prayer). Through these questions, consider the true level of intimacy you have with God in your prayer life.

Question #1: What is supposed to happen in my heart?

Prayer to God is supposed to happen in your heart. Jesus' own teaching on prayer is stated in Matthew 6 when He says,

> But thou, when thou prayest, enter into thy closet, and when thou hast shut thy door, pray to thy Father which is in secret; and thy Father which seeth in secret shall reward thee openly (v. 6).

Within our praying, ministry to God Himself is supposed to be going on. Colossians 3:16 says that we are to sing "with grace in our hearts to the Lord." Ephesians 5:19 says that we are to make "melody in your heart to the Lord." So, in the temple of our hearts, through prayer, we will be made joyful by God and see the sacrifice of our lives accepted by Him. This is based on the promise of Isaiah 56:7 which says, "Even them will I bring to my holy mountain, and make them joyful in my house of prayer: their burnt offerings and their sacrifices shall be accepted upon mine altar; for mine house shall be called an house of prayer for all people." According to Romans 12:1, even presenting our "bodies a living sacrifice, holy, acceptable unto God" is our "reasonable service" (our spiritual worship to Him.)

Question #2: What often happens in my heart?

In a word, *thieves* break in to steal prayer from the temple of my heart. Listen to God speaking in Jeremiah 7:

> Is this house which is called by my name, become a den of robbers in your eyes? Behold, even I have seen it, saith the Lord (v. 11).

In Nehemiah 13:7-12, Nehemiah, having returned to rebuild a ruined, tumbled down Jerusalem, found that an evil man had set up housekeeping for himself within the courts of the house of the Lord! Nehemiah, who was deeply grieved, threw out the man's items, cleansed the chamber, brought back the Lord's vessels, and reestablished tithing.

Have you allowed something evil to take up residence in your heart, Christ's Temple? Throw the thief out and be cleansed.

The First Thief of Prayer

What thieves are robbing you and me of our prayer life? First, there is the thief of profanity. Here, we are not talking about foul language, but making what is supposed to be holy into something common. The moneychangers that Jesus whipped and drove out of the temple had lost their respect for God's House and, therefore, profaned it. This was, and still is, unacceptable to Christ. It should be unacceptable to you and me too!

We should avoid "profane and vain babblings" (1 Timothy 6:20). We should throw out the thief of profane talk, casual attitudes about the Lord's Day, worldliness, pride, lust, selfishness, strife, and double-mindedness. Have you sanctified a special holy time and place to pray? It matters to God.

The Second Thief of Prayer

The second thief of our prayer life is well known in this 21st century. It is the thief of *busyness*—we call it the *barrenness of busyness*. This is a deception of the enemy to believe that you do not have time to pray. The truth is that we are too busy not to pray. We need our time with Jesus! If the great John Wesley felt that the busier he was, the more time he should spend in prayer, we should too.

In Luke 10:38-42, Jesus encountered two sisters— Martha, who was too busy, and Mary, who stayed in

Jesus' presence. He gave sound advice when He told Martha she was "cumbered about much serving" but that her sister Mary "had chosen that good part." Contemporary Christians must supplement their *Martha* busyness time with more *Mary* prayer time so that they become balanced.

The Third Thief of Prayer

The third thief that we have seen steal prayer intimacy with Jesus is the thief of *offense*. You cannot *lift up holy hands without wrath or doubting* (1 Timothy 2:8) if offense, anger, resentment, and unforgiveness are tolerated in your life and nurtured in your spirit. Yes, even Jesus said, "offenses will come" (Luke 17:1), but you do not have to take offense, even if it is offered to you (and Satan will see to it that it is). Offense is often born out of pain, perceived insults, unmet expectations or even jealousy. Offense and resentment prevent physical healing, keep inner peace away, and pollute your heart. Psalm 119:165 states, "Great peace have they which love thy law: and nothing shall offend them." When, in Matthew 11, Jesus sent word to a doubting, imprisoned John the Baptist, His final word of warning to the venerable prophet was, "And blessed is he, whosoever shall not be offended in me" (v. 6). Jesus was saying *John, don't take the bait of offense even when you do not understand God's ways.*

How about me? Am I offended at someone in my church? Am I offended at painful, mystifying circumstances I am facing? Perhaps I am even offended at the Lord. (Sometimes Christians who are unwilling to admit to being offended at God Himself, manifest an offended spirit toward leaders in the church.) It is time to do what Jesus did and militantly, intentionally drive away the thieves of prayer that reside in my heart. Nothing is more important than maintaining intimate closeness with God in prayer by throwing out the thieves. Sometimes the only way to keep the offense out of my heart is to have faith that God truly knows what He is doing with me.

Question #3: Finally, what does God do after my house of prayer has been cleansed, and the thieves of my prayer life have been driven out?

Simple. He will cause good things to happen in your prayer life! After Jesus threw out the thieves, Matthew 21:14 says, "And the blind and the lame came to him in the temple; and he healed them." Once the temple of prayer was clean of the thieves, sight was given to the blind. In other words, God is now free to give you a vision, wisdom you've prayed for, insight you need, direction for decisions you face, and discernment for the demonic spirits you encounter. In the now-sanctified house of prayer, Jesus made the lame to walk. This is to say that though you have been weary, heavy-laden and struggling to keep the faith, now your sanctified prayer life will receive renewed strength, fresh power, and a second wind from the Holy Spirit! It is time to rise and walk in the power of the Comforter through a renewed prayer intimacy with God.

Let's be clear, even Satan has a relationship with God. It is a rebellious, adversarial relationship. Our relationship with the Father in Heaven is of love. Jesus said in Mark 12:30, "And thou shalt love the Lord thy God with all thy heart, and with all thy soul, and with all thy mind, and with all thy strength: this is the first commandment." Your Father is waiting for you in your prayer closet.

Praying, The *Breath* of Life

My Prayers to Pray

Dear Father in Heaven, I come to You today because I want to be close to You. Father, I love You, I need You, and I want to walk in Your presence.

Dear Lord, today I want to please You. Help me to live, think, and speak in ways that will please You. I want to make You smile, and I want You to take joy in my devotion to You. I love You, dear Lord, like no other, and I cannot imagine ever living without Your precious presence.

Dear Heavenly Father, I come to You with sincere sorrow for having allowed my busyness to crowd out my priority time with You. I am sorry for allowing myself to be so casual and profane about our special time together. I admit that I have carried bitterness, offense, and unforgiveness toward others in my heart. I know that You cannot be pleased, and I am sorry for grieving Your Holy Spirit. I confess my sins and ask You to forgive me, cleanse me, and restore me. I throw these thieves out of my life so that I may have close intimacy in prayer with You my Lord. Please make my heart into Your very own temple of prayer.

Dear Father, I know that You can make me righteous because You are Jehovah Tsidqenu. I know that You can heal my body because You are Jehovah Rapha. I know that You desire to provide for all of my personal, family, and church needs because You are Jehovah Jireh. Lord, I thank You, and I love You with all of my heart.

SESSION ONE

Questions for Discussion and Reflection

1. When I pray, do I know all that the Bible teaches me about His Names? Do I understand how to apply that to my life? Do I call these Names as I pray and relate to the Lord and His character, allowing me to enter into a closer relationship with Him?

2. Do I know enough about God's character to trust Him to reveal my sins to me? Am I specific enough about my sins (unforgiveness; lust; selfishness; disobedience; worldliness; overindulgence in food, shopping, Internet, TV, etc.)?

3. Do I sometimes see praying as a chore, or do I embrace my time with the Heavenly Father as a special time for showing love to Him and being loved by Him?

4. When John Wesley said that the busier he was, the more time he should spend in prayer, which of the three thieves of prayer does this bring to mind? Discuss the danger of each of the three different thieves of prayer.

5. If someone heard my praying to God, would they get the idea that I truly love God or that I just need Him to take care of my wish list?

SESSION ONE
My Prayer Journal

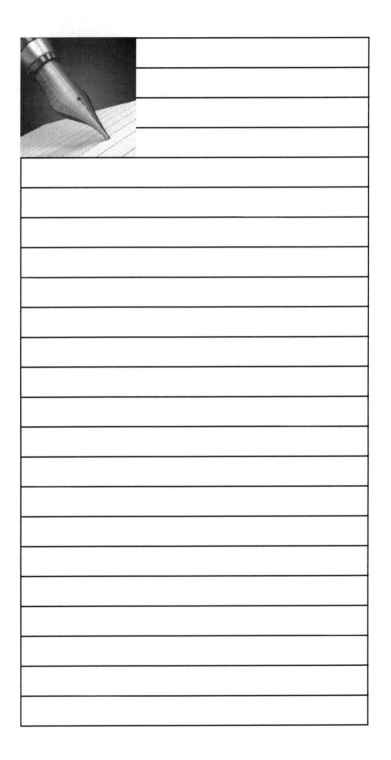

Praying, The *Breath* of Life

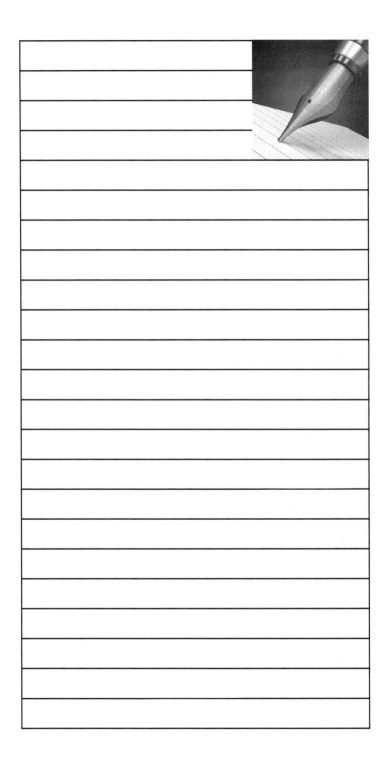

Praying

Is *Believing* God

DR. O. WAYNE BREWER

Praying, The *Breath* of Life

SESSION TWO

Scriptures

Genesis 18:14

Is anything too hard for the Lord? At the time appointed I will return unto thee, according to the time of life, and Sarah shall have a son.

2 Chronicles 20:20

. . . Jehoshaphat stood and said, Hear me, O Judah, and ye inhabitants of Jerusalem; Believe in the Lord your God, so shall ye be established; believe his prophets, so shall ye prosper.

Jeremiah 32:27

Behold, I am the Lord, the God of all flesh: is there any thing too hard for me?

Matthew 15:28

Then Jesus answered and said unto her, O woman, great is thy faith: be it unto thee even as thou wilt. And her daughter was made whole from that very hour.

Mark 9:23

Jesus said unto him, "If thou canst believe, all things are possible to him that believeth.

Luke 7:6-10

Then Jesus went with them. And when he was now not far from the house, the centurion sent friends to him, saying unto him, Lord, trouble not thyself: for I am not worthy that thou shouldest enter under my roof:

Wherefore neither thought I myself worthy to come unto thee: but say in a word and my servant shall be healed.

For I am a man set under authority, having under me soldiers, and I say unto one, Go, and he goeth; and to another, Come, and he cometh; and to my servant, Do this, and he doeth it.

When Jesus heard these things, he marveled at him, and turned him about, and said unto the people that followed him, I say unto you, I have not found so great faith, no, not in Israel.

And they that went were sent, returning to the house, found the servant whole that had been sick.

John 11:40-42, 45

Jesus saith unto her, Said I not unto thee, that, if thou wouldest believe, thou shouldest see the glory of God? Then they took away the stone from the place where the dead was laid. And Jesus lifted up his eyes, and said, Father, I thank thee that thou hast heard me.

And I knew that thou hearest me always: but because of the people which stand by I said it, that they may believe that thou hast sent me.

Then many of the Jews which came to Mary, and had seen the things which Jesus did, believed on him.

John 16:23
And in that day ye shall ask me nothing. Verily, verily, I say unto you, Whatsoever ye shall ask the Father in my name, he will give it you.

Romans 4:17-22
(As it is written, I have made thee a father of many nations,) before him who he believed, even God, who quickeneth the dead, and calleth those things which be not as though they were.

Who against hope believed in hope, that he might become the father of many nations, according to that which was spoken, So shall thy seed be.

And being not weak in faith, he considered not his own body now dead, when he was about an hundred years old, neither yet the deadness of Sarah's womb:
He staggered not at the promise of God through unbelief; but was strong in faith, giving glory to God;

And being fully persuaded that, what he had promised, he was able also to perform.

And therefore it was imputed to him for righteousness.

Romans 10:17
So then faith cometh by hearing, and hearing by the word of God.

Hebrews 10:38
Now the just shall live by faith: but if any man draw back, my soul shall have no pleasure in him.

Hebrews 11:1-2
Now faith is the substance of things hoped for, the evidence of things not seen.

For by it the elders obtained a good report.

Hebrews 11:6
But without faith it is impossible to please him: for he that cometh to God must believe that he is, and that he is a rewarder of them that diligently seek him.

Hebrews 11:8-12
By faith Abraham, when he was called to go out into a place which he should after receive for an inheritance, obeyed; and he went out, not knowing whither he went.

By faith he sojourned in the land of promise, as in a strange country, dwelling in tabernacles with Isaac and Jacob, the heirs with him of the same promise:

For he looked for a city which hath foundations, whose builder and maker is God.

Through faith also Sarah herself received strength to conceive seed, and was delivered of a child when she was past age, because she judged him faithful who had promised.

Therefore sprang there even of one, and him as good as dead, so many as the stars of the sky in multitude, and as the sand which is by the sea shore innumerable.

Praying, The *Breath* of Life

SESSION TWO

Study

IT IS INTIMACY WITH GOD that gives birth to faith. Out of our faith in Him is born a lifestyle of believing the Lord. When you pray, do you really, truly believe God and all His promises to you? So many times we pray to the Father in heaven but don't expect Him to answer us. We fall into the habit of just mouthing words to God without genuine faith.

The story is told of a children's Sunday school class that was supporting and praying for a particular missionary overseas. They had been told that he worked hard and thus was very busy. The class of youngsters wanted to communicate with the missionary and wrote a letter saying, "Dear Brother Green, we're writing to you but we don't expect you to answer us." I believe it is too often true that we pray to the Father without deeply believing that He is actually going to answer. Even though we sometimes doubt, God still says to us, "Call unto me, and I will answer thee, and show thee great and mighty things, which thou knowest not" (Jeremiah 33:3). Praying is believing God.

Prayer and Faith Go Together

Like bread and butter, prayer and faith go together. What fosters our faith in God? Believing God with great faith comes from spending intimate time with Him and in the Word. As we breathe in the Word, we will find that our breath of prayer to the Lord will increase our faith. Romans 10:17 says, "So then faith cometh by hearing, and hearing by the word of God." Belief and prayer are linked at the deepest level. In Mark 9:23, "Jesus said unto him, If thou canst believe, all things are possible to him that believeth."

It is interesting to note that just as our praise brings us peace and peace fosters praise, so does praying build our faith while our faith, in turn, strengthens our prayer life. Faith is the very essence of believing God and is an evident sign of spiritual intimacy with the Lord. When we believe God in all things at all times and circumstances, it is a testimony of the prayer life of a disciple who devotes himself (or herself) to the prayer closet.

Cooking Your Faith In Prayer

Belief in God is born in your time spent with Him in prayer. I once had the pleasure of listening to and meeting the pastor of one of the world's largest Pentecostal churches. He testified that in the early life of his congregation, he spent five hours each day in prayer ministering to the Lord. When the church attendance reached about 3,000, some of his church members insisted he spend more time ministering to them or they would stop attending the church. So he prayed about it and then told his members that they could do what they wanted but that he was going to minister to God in prayer! That was his unequivocal priority. He correctly reasoned that even God has needs since God is love and love requires fellowship. When we pray to God, we are fellowshipping with Him.

When we minister to God, said the pastor, then God will minister to people through us! This church later grew to many thousands of people. Maybe he was on to something with this whole prayer thing. I believe that the higher priority which praying has in the life of a disciple, the more that disciple tends to trust and believe God.

I heard the pastor make this humorous but profound statement: "If you are not cooked with prayer, you are raw fish—so get cooked with prayer." All too often we don't believe God for great things because our faith level in the Lord is like a plate of spiritual sushi—uncooked with prayer!

The Faith Factor: Prayer That Pleases God Also Believes God

Do you want the kind of prayer life that sees miracles and pleases God? There is a key to moving the hand of God (miracles) and touching the heart of God (pleasing Him), and that key is *faith*! For the disciple of Christ, prayer that believes God is prayer that has faith in God. Our breath of life bears fruit when we have faith. Hebrews 11 states plainly,

But without faith it is impossible to please him: for he that cometh to God must *believe* that he is, and that he is a rewarder of them that diligently seek him (v. 6 italics added).

Look at the Gospels. Faith is what brought about miracle after miracle and in so doing, moved the hand of God. Likewise, faith (according to Hebrews 11:6), is what touches the heart of God by pleasing Him. If you please God by praying with faith, it doesn't really matter who else you displease. If, however, you displease God with prayers void of faith, then it no longer matters who else you do please. C. H. Spurgeon[1] once said, "Little faith will bring your soul to heaven, but great faith will bring heaven to your soul." Faith is the birthmark of a disciple of Christ.

Why Our Praying Must Believe God

Believing God is the essence of our praying. In the New Testament, the saved were called "believers" before they were called "Christians." John 6:29 says, "Jesus answered and said unto them, This is the work of God, that ye believe on him whom he hath sent." Think about it, the greatest sin, other than blaspheming the Holy Spirit, is unbelief. The reason the Hebrews had to spend another 40 years in the wilderness was because 10 of the 12 spies sent into the Promised Land allowed their fears to cause

---

1   Morning and Evening: A New Edition of the Classic Devotional Based on the Holy Bible, English Standard Version

them to sin through unbelief.

Speaking of the Holy Spirit, John 16:8, 9 says that "And when he is come, he will reprove the world of sin, and of righteousness, and of judgement: of sin, because they believe not on me." People are going to hell because they do not believe. John 3:18 says, "He that believeth on him is not condemned, but he that believeth not is condemned already . . ." Unbelief is the source of all other sins. Adam and Eve sinned in the Garden of Eden because they did not believe what God had said. Praise God that the Christian life is to be lived by faith. According to Hebrews 10:38, "Now the just shall live by faith . . ." Praying is believing God!

A Man Called Abraham

In God's wonderful School of Faith, in which all Christians are enrolled, God is the Principal, the Bible is the curriculum, and Abraham is the star student. This man, known as the friend of God in James 2:23, was intimately close with God precisely because he was a man of faith who believed Him.

Four millennia ago an old man, a heathen named Abram, lived in Ur of the Chaldees and was enrolled in God's School of Faith. Abram, later renamed Abraham (meaning *father of a multitude*) was the husband of Sarai (meaning *contentiousness*), who was later renamed Sarah (meaning *princess*). He was a pilgrim who was traveling to a destination unknown to him. He was walking by faith because the Lord did not tell him where he was going to travel or what he would experience along the way.

Abraham's story is a story of one of the elders who by faith "obtained a good report," as Hebrews 11:2 says. He received an "A" on his believing God report card. Over and over again, above all else, he had faith in God. For this reason he was considered by God a friend. God spoke to this old man and his barren, old wife and revealed to them that they would have a son and become parents to a multitude. It was humanly impossible and yet Abraham pleased God by believing Him without reservation.

The Lord will engineer situations in your life that will challenge your prayer life to breathe faith, even great faith. It is said that the great Christian, George Mueller, wrote in the margin of his Bible next to Psalm 37:23 ("The steps of a good man are ordered by the Lord . . . ")—"and the stops also."[2] God engineers both our steps and our stops. God is at work in your life stretching your faith. Perhaps, like Abraham, you are faced with your own weaknesses and limitations. For Abraham, it was his old age. It may be that you are faced with a Sarai (barren and contentious) situation that seems to contend with the faith you are trying to muster.

The challenges we face seem to argue with the promises and goodness of God. For this reason, we cannot walk by

2   "Streams in the Desert" devotional, *Ordering the Stops* by Mrs. Charles E. Cowman

sight but by faith in God alone. Let's look at Paul's brief but inspiring description of the faith of Abraham our spiritual father.

> (As it is written, "I have made thee a father of many nations,) before him whom he believed, even God, who quickeneth the dead, and calleth those things which be not as though they were. Who against hope believed in hope, that he might become the father of many nations, according to that which was spoken, So shall thy seed be. And being not weak in faith, he considered not his own body now dead, when he was about an hundred years old, neither yet the deadness of Sarah's womb: He staggered not at the promise of God through unbelief; but was strong in faith, giving glory to God; And being fully persuaded that, what he had promised, he was able also to perform. And therefore it was imputed to him for righteousness (Romans 4:17-22).

Believing God in prayer means having faith that knows God calls "those things which be not as though they were" (v. 17). Believing God in prayer means being strong in faith and not considering your own limitations or the contrary, challenging aspects of your situation (v. 19). Believing God in prayer means not staggering in doubt at God's promises, but rather glorifying and praising God even before you see His promises fulfilled in your life (v. 20). Believing God in prayer means "being fully persuaded" that God is able to perform what He promised.

For all of these reasons we can say Abraham indeed believed God and as a result of his unwavering faith, God considered him righteous (v. 22). No wonder Abraham was a friend of God. The Lord, however, is not just a friend of Abraham, but of countless more who love, believe, and pray to a Heavenly Father they know is the living God of love and of all power in heaven and in earth. The Lord desires your friendship. In John 15:15 Jesus said, "but I have called you friends; for all things I have heard of my Father I have made known unto you." Friends trust and believe. Today, Jesus is inviting you to a rich, intimate prayer life of believing Him as His beloved friend.

To Believe Or Not To Believe

If prayer is to truly be the *breath of life* in my walk with Christ, I must first ask myself this question: will I believe or will I not believe? How you answer this question charts the course of your prayer life and indeed, your very salvation. After Jesus' resurrection from the tomb, all of the disciples saw Jesus alive again (John 20:19-20) except for two. One was Judas Iscariot and he was now dead. The other disciple who had not seen Jesus was Thomas, who had not been present with the others. When told of the resurrected Lord, he responded,

> Except I shall see in his hands the print of the nails, and put my finger into the print of the nails, and

thrust my hand into his side, I will not believe (John 20:25).

Eight days later the Lord appeared to all the disciples, including Thomas. Having put his finger and his hand into Jesus' wounds, Thomas exclaimed, "My Lord and my God!" Jesus, noting that Thomas believed because he had seen with his physical eyes, said, "blessed are they that have not seen, and yet have believed" (John 20:29).

At an earlier time (in John 11) we witness Jesus again striving to teach His followers to believe. After being urgently summoned to come heal his dear friend Lazarus, the Lord intentionally took His time in arriving on the scene. By the time He got there *sick Lazarus* was now *dead Lazarus*—and four days dead at that! Many Jews at the time believed that the soul of the dead would depart the body after three days. Lazarus' four days of death whispered the words "too late" to Lazarus' sisters, Martha and Mary. In fact, the rest of the mourners had already given up hope. Listen to the emphasis on believing in the following conversation between Jesus and Martha in John 11:

> Jesus saith unto her, Thy brother shall rise again. Martha saith unto him, I know that he shall rise again in the resurrection at the last day. Jesus said unto her, I am the resurrection, and the life: he that believeth in me, though he were dead, yet shall he live: And whosoever liveth and believeth in me shall never die. Believest thou this? She saith unto

him, Yea, Lord: I believe that thou art the Christ, the Son of God, which should come into the world (vv. 23-27).

Like many of us Martha believed He was Lord (phase one faith), and that had He been there earlier He could have healed Lazarus (phase two faith). However, when it came to phase three faith, which makes the impossible become possible, Martha struggled a bit more, but still acknowledged He was the Messiah.

When you are praying, is your faith at phase one (Jesus I know You are Lord), at phase two (Jesus I know You can help and heal), or is it at phase three (Jesus, You are the Lord of all flesh and there is nothing too hard for You, according to Jeremiah 32:27)? You can have phase three faith if you will only believe God when you pray!

After Jesus called Lazarus forth out of the tomb, He emphasized to the onlookers how important believing God really is. John 11:40 says,

Jesus saith unto her, Said I not unto thee, that, if thou wouldest believe, thou shouldest see the glory of God?

Getting The Job Done In Prayer

There is no question about it, prayer is work. Prayer is labor. Prayer is what gets the divine direction for a decision, the mountain moved, and everything accomplished that is subject to prayer. However, you are not alone.

Remember that true praying is both personal and corporate (believers praying together, in one mind and one purpose). Examples in the Bible of corporate praying are 2 Chronicles 6 and 7, Ezra 8, and Acts 2. Praying with other believers is powerful, and you will witness God perform miracles as He responds to the unified petitions of His people! (See Appendix Five, *Five Biblical Elements of Corporate Prayer.*)

Praying in the Spirit

According to Paul, the Holy Spirit helps us pray. One of the great benefits of being baptized in the Holy Spirit is the gift of tongues. While it is true that there is much more to gain from the Baptism of the Holy Spirt, God does not minimize the importance of this gift. He obviously thinks speaking in tongues when we pray is a great help to us. He inspired Paul to devote 1 Corinthians 14, virtually an entire chapter, to tongues. You cannot find an entire chapter on water baptism or tithing—although both are important. God does not devote biblical teaching to insignificant things that have no ultimate purpose.

Yes, tongues is important to God and should be important to you and your prayer life. Tongues takes our prayer life to a higher and farther-reaching dimension, even more in tune with God's perfect will. Please understand, tongues is not a substitute for prayer but it is a part of prayer.

Let's look at the following verses in 1 Corinthians 14:

For he that speaketh in an unknown tongue speaketh not unto men, but unto God: for no man understandeth him; howbeit in the spirit he speaketh mysteries (v. 2).

He that speaketh in an unknown tongue edifieth himself; but he that prophesieth edifieth the church (v. 4).

I thank my God, I speak with tongues more than ye all (v. 18).

The Apostle here is speaking of unknown tongues primarily in a Spirit-filled believer's private prayer life, not tongues in a public assembly where there would usually be an interpretation. The Holy Spirit helps us to pray, which strengthens our faith. Paul said,

Likewise the Spirit also helpeth our infirmities: for we know not what we should pray for as we ought: but the Spirit itself maketh intercession for us with groanings which cannot be uttered (Romans 8:26).

My own father has never shied away from the gift of tongues or the labor of praying. I have witnessed many of his faith-filled prayers answered by God, often to my own personal benefit. Praise God!

Praying in the Spirit edifies, strengthens, and recharges your spiritual battery. Jude 1:20 says, "But ye, beloved, building up yourselves on your most holy faith, praying in the Holy Ghost." The cares of life and the opposition of the enemy tend to tear you down, but both Apostles Paul and Jude teach that praying in tongues actually builds you up "on your most holy faith."

I have found that when the Holy Spirit speaks/prays through me in tongues that He is letting me know He is right there with me. When He witnesses through me in tongues to God, I sense my bond with the Heavenly Father lovingly, intimately strengthened. God intended for all His children to enjoy the baptism of the Holy Spirit for so many reasons, not the least of which is to support our praying. I do not have to speak in tongues to pray, but it is a gift from God. I don't want to refuse a gift from my Heavenly Father.

Establishing My Prayer of Faith

Believing God in prayer is having faith in Him, that He is a rewarder of those who diligently seek Him. There are several factors which assist the prayer warrior in believing that God will send the answer.

First, we know God is a prayer-answering God. With great assurance David said in Psalm 4:3, "But know that the Lord hath set apart him that is godly for himself: the Lord will hear when I call unto him." Micah said, "Therefore I will look unto the Lord; I will wait for the God of my salvation: my God will hear me" (Micah 7:7).

Second, we ask in accordance with God's will. While it is possible to pray amiss (for fulfillment of foolish lusts, for example), we know there are prayers which are always God's will—for God to be glorified, sinners to be saved, the discouraged to be encouraged, and so much more.

Third, we have the assurance of the Holy Spirit that helps us to believe God in prayer. An earlier generation of Pentecostal Christians called this *praying through*. Sometimes this comes after much diligent prayer and sometimes this comes more quickly, as when the charismatic *gift of faith* is in operation and the believer is fully assured that God has heard and answered the supplication.

Fourth, our prayer is often characterized by the genuine travail of labor as a woman in childbirth. The travail of prayer finds its sweetest moment when the answer actually arrives. As a mother brings a child into existence, so prayer that believes God brings God's will and wonder into any situation that we may face.

One day Jesus was teaching His disciples that a time would come that He would no longer be with them. In John 16:23 He said, "And in that day ye shall ask me nothing. Verily, verily, I say unto you, Whatsoever ye shall ask the Father in my name, he will give it you." This passage turns our prayer of believing into a prayer of giving thanks to God!

Praying, The *Breath* of Life

My Prayers to Pray

Lord Jesus, Your Word invites me to call out to You and You will answer me and show me great and mighty things. Today, the greatest, mightiest thing I can imagine is seeing You. Help me to see You and understand You in an intimate way. I'm believing You for this today.

Dear Lord, I want to believe You for great things. Part of me completely believes and trusts You. But Lord, please help the part of me that doubts. Help me to keep my eyes on You and not on the storms that are blowing over my life today.

Dear Father, I want to be Your friend like Abraham is Your friend. Help my faith to be complete as Abraham's faith. Help me not to stagger in doubt at Your promises, or to meditate on my own weaknesses and the contrary nature of my tough situation. Help me to give glory to You and have genuine faith, even before I see the answer.

Lord Jesus, sometimes I feel so unworthy and undeserving. Help me to believe in Your grace and Your love. Please let me enjoy even the crumbs which fall from Your table.

O Lord, I thank You for the gift of the Holy Spirit. I thank You for the Comforter who walks alongside me every day and encourages me, illuminates me, and anoints me. Please baptize me in the Holy Spirit because if You want me to have Your gift, then I know that I want to receive it from You. Speak through me precious Holy Spirit. I praise You. I love You. I welcome You. My heart is Your temple. Welcome Holy Spirit!

I declare that I believe Your promise that if I ask anything of the Father in the Name of Jesus, then You will give it to me. I believe You Lord. I want what You want. I praise You for Your answer and Your provision even before I see it!

Questions for Discussion and Reflection

1. Has God called me to something that seems impossible given my current situation? How can I look to the life of Abraham as an example of believing God no matter what?

2. If someone overheard me praying, would they get the idea that I truly believed God was going to answer me, or that I was just mouthing words without any real expectation of an answer from heaven?

3. What do you think is meant when the pastor said, "If you are not cooked with prayer, you are raw fish"? Do I sometimes feel like my faith in God is spiritual sushi? If so, how can I commit to cooking my prayers?

4. When Jesus asked them to roll away the stone from the grave, Martha said, "Lord, by this time he stinketh" (John 11:39). Do you think that believers today sometimes try to tell the Lord their situation stinks so bad that even He cannot help them? Why do we doubt?

5. If "faith comes by hearing and hearing by the Word of God" (Romans 10:17 NKJV), am I truly placing enough importance on being in church to hear the word preached, taught, and sung? Am I breathing in faith-building Scriptures so that I can breathe out faith-filled prayer?

6. Am I willing to learn and memorize faith Scriptures so that I can pray them out loud when I am talking to God?

SESSION TWO

My Prayer Journal

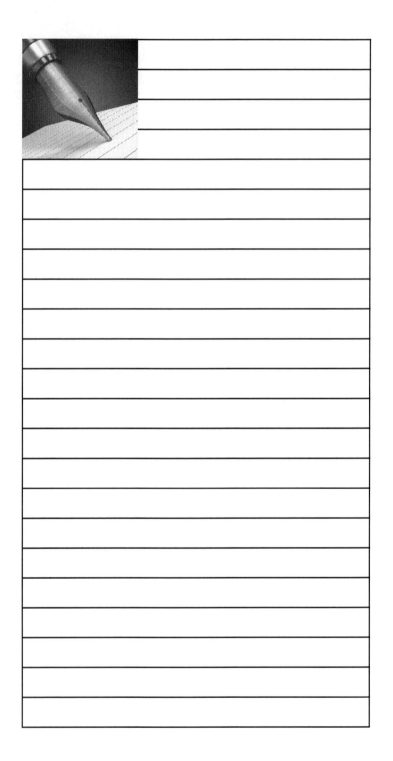

Praying, The *Breath* of Life

Praying
Is *Giving Thanks* to God

PAMELA R. BREWER

Praying, The *Breath* of Life

SESSION THREE

Scriptures

Psalm 100:4
Enter into his gates with thanksgiving, and into his courts with praise: be thankful unto him, and bless his name.

Psalm 105:1-6
O give thanks unto the Lord; call upon his name: make known his deeds among the people.

Sing unto him, sing psalms unto him: talk ye of all his wondrous works.

Glory ye in his holy name: let the heart of them rejoice that seek the Lord.

Seek the Lord, and his strength: seek his face evermore.

Remember his marvelous works that he hath done; his wonders, and the judgments of his mouth;

O ye seed of Abraham his servant, ye children of Jacob his chosen.

Psalm 116:17-18
I will offer to thee the sacrifice of thanksgiving, and will call upon the name of the Lord.

I will pay my vows unto the Lord now in the presence of all his people.

Psalm 136:1-3

O give thanks unto the Lord; for he is good: for his mercy endureth for ever.

O give thanks unto the God of gods: for his mercy endureth for ever.

O give thanks to the Lord of lords: for his mercy endureth for ever.

Luke 1:46-55

And Mary said, My soul doth magnify the Lord,

And my spirit hath rejoiced in God my Saviour.

For he hath regarded the low estate of his handmaiden: for, behold, from henceforth all generations shall call me blessed.

For he that is mighty hath done to me great things; and holy is his name.

And his mercy is on them that fear him from generation to generation.

He hath shewed strength with his arm; he hath scattered the proud in the imagination of their hearts.

He hath put down the mighty from their seats, and exalted them of low degree.

He hath filled the hungry with good things; and the rich he hath sent empty away.
He hath helped his servant Israel, in remembrance of his mercy;

As he spake to our fathers, to Abraham, and to his seed
for ever.

Luke 2:36-38
And there was one Anna, a prophetess, the daughter of
Phanuel, of the tribe of Aser: she was of a great age, and
had lived with an husband seven years from her virginity;

And she was a widow of about fourscore and four years,
which departed not from the temple, but served God
with fastings and prayers night and day.

And she coming in that instant gave thanks likewise unto
the Lord, and spake of him to all them that looked for
redemption in Jerusalem.

John 12:1-8
Then Jesus six days before the passover came to Bethany,
where Lazarus was, which had been dead, whom he
raised from the dead.

There they made him a supper; and Martha served: but
Lazarus was one of them that sat at the table with him.

Then took Mary a pound of ointment of spikenard, very
costly, and anointed the feet of Jesus, and wiped his feet
with her hair: and the house was filled with the odour of
the ointment.

Then saith one of his disciples, Judas Iscariot, Simon's
son, which should betray him,
Why was not this ointment sold for three hundred pence,
and given to the poor?

This he said, not that he cared for the poor; but because he was a thief, and had the bag, and bare what was put therein.

Then said Jesus, Let her alone: against the day of my burying hath she kept this.

For the poor always ye have with you; but me ye have not always.

Colossians 2:6-7
As ye have therefore received Christ Jesus the Lord, so walk ye in him:

Rooted and built up in him, and stablished in the faith, as ye have been taught, abounding therein with thanksgiving.

Praying, The *Breath* of Life

SESSION THREE

Study

TO BE JESUS' DISCIPLE IS TO EXPERIENCE the free flow of thanksgiving in prayer. Giving thanks to God is not a mere add-on to our prayer life. In fact, Colossians 2:6-7 declares that the disciple of Jesus is to *abound* in thanksgiving! With this Scripture teaching in mind, let's pause and take stock of what we have so far experienced in prayer. Because we are intimate with God in prayer, we know Him (session 1). When we pray in faith, trusting in God and all that His Word says, we believe Him (session 2). Therefore, as disciples of Christ we can in all things and through all things, at all times, give Him thanks. We know that He loves us. His thoughts toward us are greater than the sands in the sea. He is a good God, who loves us so much that He sent His Son Jesus Christ for our salvation. He gave up His very best for us and continues to make way for our healing, deliverance, salvation, and wisdom. He truly is all we need.

The Prayer of Thanksgiving Rests in God's Goodness

The prayer of thanksgiving is a time of peace and restful breathing. Try it even now. Think of something you are thankful for—maybe a grandchild, health, or salvation. Feel the breath of peace wash over you. When, as Christians, we recognize how thankful we are to God for every good thing that comes from Him, we are showing God our trust in Him. Your mind is where most battles are lost or won. When we refocus our mind on God, through the prayer of thanksgiving, we become victorious over the lies of Satan.

The Bible tells us in 1 John 4:18, "There is no fear in love; but perfect love casteth out fear: because fear hath torment. He that feareth is not made perfect in love." This love that is being spoken of is not dependent upon *us* having perfect love, rather *it rests upon the perfect love that God our Father has for each of His children.* I love the meaning of the Greek word that is used here for "casts out," *ballo.* It means to fling violently, throw out, to drive out. It's not a halfway job; it is complete. It's out of here!

There is something special about prayerfully giving thanks to God, who focuses our heart upon Him and casts out our fear. Thanksgiving interwoven in your prayers will bring rest into your weary heart, even in the stormiest of times. Prayers of thanksgiving will remind you of who you depend upon, and will cast out your doubts as you realize it is His power and for His glory that you move and have your being.

The Prayer of Thanksgiving Recognizes God's Goodness

As believers, we can rest in the goodness of God.

We should be thankful for who we are in Christ: 2 Corinthians 5:17—a new creature; 1 Peter 2:9—a royal priesthood; Ephesians 2:10—His workmanship created in Christ Jesus; 2 Corinthians 5:21—the righteousness of God; John 1:12—children of God; and the list goes on.

The prayer breath of thanks recognizes how good God is and what He has done for us. Mary, the mother of Jesus, went from being a single virgin engaged to Joseph, to being the mother of the Savior of the world. The first time we are introduced to Mary is in Luke 1:27. Note the trust Mary had when she responded to the angel in Luke 1:38. When he told her she would become pregnant with the Savior of the world, she responded "Behold the handmaid of the Lord; be it unto me according to thy word." She could have said, "No, not me, think of the shame, I have my life all planned." She could have doubted that the angel was real or even from the Lord and rejected his words. Thank the Lord, she humbled herself, gave herself completely to Him, and submitted to His will for her life. *Mary recognized the great perfect love of the Lord toward her* as the angel told her in Luke 1.

Hail, thou that art highly favored, the Lord is with thee: blessed art thou among women (Luke 1:28).

There's so much to consider as we look at Luke 1:39-45. Verse 39 paints a beautiful picture of Mary's response as she is filled with joy. She runs to the hill country of Judah. Then when Mary sees Elisabeth (who is pregnant with John the Baptist), Scriptures tell us in verse 41, "And it came to pass, that, when Elisabeth heard the salutation of Mary, the babe leaped in her womb; and Elisabeth was filled with the Holy Ghost:"

This breath of joyful thanks springs forth from Elisabeth as she too gives praise and thanksgiving. When the breath of thanks is in our lives, it will cause others to join us in thanks and praise. Have you ever noticed, while partaking in a worship service, that thanksgiving and praise have a contagious quality? Elisabeth, who was carrying her own miracle, the forerunner of our Lord, was filled with the Holy Ghost!

The breath of praise spread peace, joy, hope, love, and promise. Not only did Mary receive a glorious, *impossible* promise, but so did Elisabeth. Two miracle births, two promises fulfilled, two women willing to believe the promises of the Lord, were now thanking Him as they proclaimed His goodness! There are so many other choices that these two women could have made in their minds and hearts. However, *they chose to believe the Word of God that had been brought to them and then gave thanks and began to proclaim His Word.*

Luke 1:46-55 records the Song of Mary. It is here that young Mary's heart pours out a beautiful song of thanksgiving. Here we see an anointing to pray a prayer of thanksgiving to God. She humbles herself but exalts Him. The *breath of thanks will cause us to see beyond our circumstances.* Instead of focusing on the fact that she was pregnant before she was even married, Mary trusted the Lord. Both Mary and Elisabeth saw the majesty, mercy, strength, righteousness, judgement, provisions, and promises of God!

The Prayer of Thanksgiving Receives God's Goodness

When Mary humbled herself and trusted the Word of God sent by an angel, she received blessings greater than she could have ever imagined. In Luke 1:28, the angel said, "Rejoice, highly favored one, the Lord is with you; blessed are you among women!" In verse 30, the angel again says to her, ". . . for you have found favor with God." The favor of God is a wonderful reality! *The prayer breath of thanks receives His Goodness.*

When Mary received His goodness, she received the praises from Elisabeth who proclaimed in Luke 1:45, "And blessed is she that believed: for there shall be a performance of those things which were told her from the Lord." Because Mary believed, she received the promise! This caused Elisabeth to magnify the Lord. Furthermore, Mary began to thank the Lord and in Luke 1:48 began to prophesy her own future! Have you ever thanked God in advance? This is something my husband and I routinely do in our prayers.

The Scriptures are full of promises for healing from every disease and brokenness, deliverance, salvation for our children and grandchildren—even resurrection when things are already dead. God wants us to believe Him! He has already given these things to us. Just as the angel told Mary the good news, His written Word proclaims the good news of His promises to us today. Mary declared in verse 48 that she who was just minutes before a mere handmaiden, will forevermore be called blessed because of what God did in her when she *believed and received Him.* This is transforming power that moves you from your own plans to a greater calling and blessing from the Lord that will last forevermore!

As a young girl growing up in a non-Christian family, I read Acts 16:31, "And they said, Believe on the Lord Jesus Christ, and thou shalt be saved, and thy house." At the department store where I worked, I would pray during my break times and thank the Lord *in advance* for saving my family.

Fourteen years later, I was met at my father's funeral by a lady from the church I attended while I was growing up. She told me how just a month before my father's death, she ran into him at the same store and asked him if he was a Christian. As he told her "no," tears streamed down his face. She and my father stood there, in the very same place where I had given thanks to God for the salvation of my household, and he prayed the sinner's prayer. God is faithful!

When God speaks to us, our response should be the prayer of thanksgiving and expectation. What a wonderful, loving Heavenly Father that would bring salvation to my earthly father in the very place where He had led me to that promise, and where I received it into my spirit and thanked Him in advance. God knew even before I prayed the first prayer where and when He would save my father. What must He have been thinking as He saw me grab hold of His promise? God is so good to us!

When we are intimate with God, know Him, believe Him, and trust Him, we can then receive His goodness. The enemy of our soul wants to steal that from us. Don't let him! Once, while praying with a lady to accept Christ as her Savior, we could see that she was struggling to receive the truth that the Father in Heaven loved her enough to save her. When we asked her about her earthly Father, we immediately realized what was hindering her from receiving God and all that He had for her life. Her earthly father had been abusive—often striking her—and was very strict. It was hard for her to receive the concept of a loving father. When we have a true picture of who our Heavenly Father is and of His great love in the sacrifice of His Son, Jesus Christ, for our sins, we can receive the breath of His goodness into our own lives while at the same time pouring out our thanksgiving on Him.

John 12:1-8 gives a beautiful example of another Mary as she thankfully received the goodness of the Lord. Mary was so filled with thanks that it caused her to dramatically pour out a very expensive perfume upon the Lord Jesus as she anointed His feet and then wiped them with her own hair. This breath of thanks filled the room with a sweet fragrance. Just a few days earlier, Jesus had raised her brother Lazarus from the dead. Now Mary, filled with gratitude, sacrificed this very expensive perfume in order to anoint the Lord of Life with the costly sacrifice of her thanksgiving. Mary had received the goodness of the Lord into her own life. From her love and thankfulness for Him, she poured out her perfume, anointed the Lord, and blessed Him. Mary had freely received the Lord's goodness and responded with her own extravagant thanksgiving. Jesus was deeply moved.

Indeed, Jesus exclaimed in Matthew 26:13, "Verily I say unto you, Wheresoever this gospel shall be preached in the whole world, there shall also this, that this woman hath done, be told for a memorial of her." Unquestionably, our prayer breath of thanksgiving means so very much to our Lord.

The Prayer of Thanksgiving Restates God's Goodness

Finally, when we breathe the prayer of thanksgiving we restate His love and endless mercy. We are setting ourselves in agreement with God's Word and God's goodness. Some of the most powerful prayers of thanksgiving you can offer are prayers that quote thanksgiving Scriptures back to Him and remember past mercies He has shown you in your own life! In other words, recount back to Him the times in your life where He forgave you, healed you, provided for you, guided you, and dealt tenderly with you. As a disciple of Christ, you should devote a sizable portion of your prayer life to restating God's goodness. If someone else hears you, then so much the better! Thanksgiving praying is powerful precisely because we *overcome by the word of our testimony.*

Unlike several lepers whom Jesus healed who failed to remember to thank Him, Mary, the sister of Lazarus, did not fail to remember to give a rich sacrifice of thanksgiving to her Lord. Do you remember when He saved you? When He healed you, blessed you, had mercy on you, and called you His own? Mary did not yet know all that Jesus was to become to her in her eternal life. How could she know? She did know, however, that the Lord had delivered her out of her life of sin and raised Lazarus from the dead. That was the focus of her highest love and gratitude.

Jesus saw the heart of Mary as He compared it with the heart of Judas, who was filled with greed instead of thankfulness. Jesus also saw the busyness of Martha. Mary made the better choice that was pleasing to the Lord. The spirits of greed and busyness will cause a person to turn toward their own selfish desires, forgetting all that the Lord has done in their life and all He has promised.

However, the prayer breath of thanks to the Lord causes us to remember and to want to give all that we have to bless Him. It is a choice that all of us make each day. Will we be obedient and bring to the Lord what is already His: our time, tithes, and talents? Will we give freely and abundantly the things that He has first given to us, even though sometimes very costly? Or, will we turn our hearts toward our own selfish desires—even masking them by saying it is for others, as Judas did when he acted as though he was concerned for the poor? If we choose the heart of Judas, we have chosen the road to regret, disappointment, and death. To choose to breathe the breath of thanks to the Lord brings peace, joy, liberty, and deliverance. It even brings the anointing fragrance of the Lord into our lives and the lives of others. As disciples of Christ, let us be like the prophetess Anna in Luke 2:38 and give thanks to the Lord and speak of Jesus to all of those who look for redemption.

Psalm 107:1-6, declares God's love and mercy as our own. It says that the Lord delivers us out of our own distresses, to move us beyond our circumstances, and to give us the promises and provisions that He has waiting for us today. Breathe this prayer of thanks as we join the Psalmist in saying:

> O give thanks unto the Lord, for he is good: for his mercy endureth for ever. Let the redeemed of the Lord say so, whom he hath redeemed from the hand of the enemy; And gathered them out of the lands, from the east, and from the west, from the north, and from the south. They wandered in the wilderness in a solitary way; they found no city to dwell in. Hungry and thirsty, their soul fainted in

them. Then they cried unto the Lord in their trouble, and he delivered them out of their distresses (Psalm 107:1-6).

God already has the promised land waiting for us, filled with grapes, milk and honey, and blessings even above our needs.

I'm reminded of a recent true report of a young student from Lee University who went on a missions trip. Someone in his group had taken along one bag of about 30 large marshmallows. When he arrived at the South Sudan orphanage and saw how many children were there (130), he realized that what he had to offer was not enough. The native missionary saw the young student as he tried to put the bag away. The missionary, who knew of the goodness of the Lord for these children, encouraged the student to pray and ask the Lord to bless his small offering. As the student prayed, he considered in his heart that the children did not *need* the marshmallows. He confessed that because it was not a need but just an added blessing, his prayer was half-hearted with inner conflict. He was, however, obedient to the missionary who believed.

After the student prayed, the missionary encouraged him to begin to hand out a marshmallow to each child. Much to his surprise, there was not just enough for each child to have one, but two and three marshmallows as God miraculously multiplied them within the bag! After having witnessed such a loving miracle, this young student began to understand more fully the heart and character of his Abba Father. What a good God! What a mighty God! He can multiply whatever He desires to in order to provide for and bless His own.

Thank You Father that You don't just give us what we need, but that You love to bless Your children. Thank You Father, for those that will believe, even in the situations and circumstances that seem impossible for us.

Why breathe these prayers of thanks? Psalm 100 shows us that as we enter into His gates with thanksgiving (v. 4) we recognize that the Lord is God (v. 3), He made us and we belong to Him (v. 5). He is good, His mercy is everlasting, and His promises are for us and all the generations of our families! Furthermore, prayer through the gates of thanksgiving leads us into the courts of praise where many battles are won!

Praying, The *Breath* of Life

SESSION THREE

My Prayers to Pray

Dear Lord, help me to understand that Your ways, thoughts, and plans for me, my family, and my church are higher than I can even imagine. Help me to receive Your will into my life, the lives of my family, friends, and even my church when I don't understand it. Help me to know Your voice, dear Lord, and to recognize when I'm trying to impose my own limited knowledge and understanding, thus limiting or hindering You and Your desires. Thank You, Lord, that even when I mess up, You are so kind and will help me to find my way as I seek You! I love You Lord and thank You for hearing my prayers. I thank You for loving me so much that You, the Lord who created everything, would even know the number of hairs on my head. You know me better than I know myself.

Thank You Lord for saving my family members. Thank You for Your love in the great sacrifice of Your Son Jesus Christ for all of our sins. Thank You Lord for Your healing power over all of our diseases. Thank You Lord for sending Jesus to show us the way to live as Your children. Thank You for always hearing me and for letting me call You my Father and my Friend.

Thank You Lord for letting me see the lost through Your loving eyes of compassion. Lord, thank You that as I reach out to lost and hurting people that You have given me the power through the Holy Spirit to speak hope, life, and even the prayers that will lead them to salvation. Thank You that I don't have to depend upon my own self when situations seem impossible, as You taught us through the lives of Mary and Elisabeth. I trust You Lord and thank You that the people and things You allow in my life will always bless me and glorify You.

Questions for Discussion and Reflection

1. When is the last time I prayed a prayer of thanksgiving to God? Are prayers of thanksgiving a regular part of my daily life? How can I thank God for His goodness to me, my family, and church?

2. When I pray, do I spend 70% of my time worshipping God and enjoying Him and about 30% of my time making my requests/needs known to Him, or do I spend 30% worshipping God and 70% making my requests known?

3. When was the last time I publicly testified of my thanks to the Lord for His goodness to me and my family?

4. Do I look to God's Word for His promises for my life? Am I willing to receive His promises and begin to thank God for them even before I see the answer?

5. How do I pray the Scriptures and proclaim them over situations in my life and the lives of those that I love?

How much time do I spend meditating upon His Word and putting it in my heart?

6. How do I view my heavenly Father? Do I trust Him and believe that His Word wants to speak into my life and the life of my family and church? Can I receive what God is saying to me through His Word?

7. Would a trip to a foreign country or to a nursing home or a hospice rekindle the warm glow of thanksgiving to the Lord in my prayer life?

SESSION THREE

My Prayer Journal

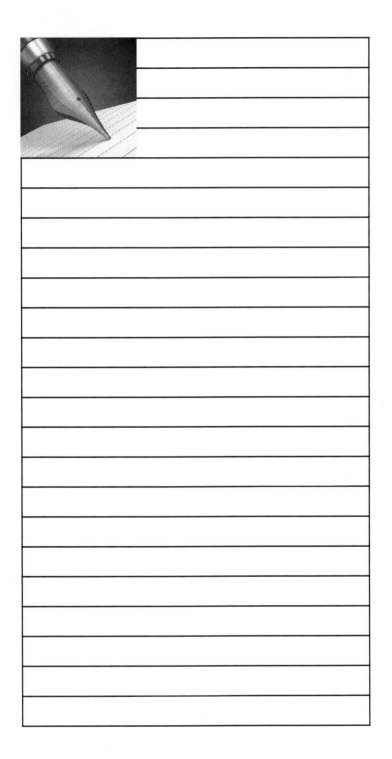

Praying, The *Breath* of Life

Praying
Is *Praising God*

PAMELA R. BREWER

Praying, The *Breath* of Life

SESSION FOUR

Scriptures

Psalm 34:1

I will bless the Lord at all times; His praise shall continually be in my mouth.

Psalm 57:7 (NKJV)

My heart is steadfast, O God, my heart is steadfast! I will sing and make melody!

Psalm 108:2-3

Awake, psaltery and harp: I myself will awake early,

I will praise Thee, O Lord, among the people: and I will sing praises to thee among the nations.

Psalm 63:3-5

Because thy lovingkindness is better than life, my lips shall praise thee.

Thus will I bless thee while I live: I will lift up my hands in thy name.

My soul shall be satisfied as with marrow and fatness; and my mouth shall praise thee with joyful lips:

Psalm 86:12

I will praise thee, O Lord my God, with all my heart: and I will glorify thy name for evermore.

Psalm 146:2 (NKJV)

While I live will I praise the Lord: I will sing praises unto my God while I have my being.

Psalm 150

Praise ye the Lord. Praise God in his sanctuary: praise him in the firmament of his power.

Praise him for his mighty acts: praise him according to his excellent greatness.
Praise him with the sound of the trumpet: praise him with the psaltery and harp.

Praise him with the timbrel and dance: praise him with stringed instruments and organs.

Praise him upon the loud cymbals: praise him upon the high sounding cymbals.

Let every thing that hath breath praise the Lord. Praise ye the Lord.

Philippians 4:4-8

Rejoice in the Lord always: and again I say, Rejoice.

Let your gentleness be known to all men. The Lord is at hand.

Be anxious for nothing, but in everything by prayer and supplication, with thanksgiving, let your requests be made known to God;

and the peace of God, which surpasses all understanding, will guard your hearts and minds through Christ Jesus.

Finally, brethren, whatever things are true, whatever things are noble, whatever things are just, whatever things are pure, whatever things are lovely, whatever things are of good report, if there is any virtue and if there is anything praiseworthy—meditate on these things

Praying, The *Breath* of Life

SESSION FOUR

Study

WHEN WE PRAY, WE ENTER INTO HIS "gates with thanksgiving" (Psalm 100:4), but it is with praise that we press closer into the courts of His Presence. Thanksgiving is often our expression to God for what He has already done for us and others. When we praise God, we are expressing adoration toward Him for who He is, and sometimes for what we believe He is going to do in the future. We can praise Him for who He Is when we read the Word of God and spend time with Him in prayer.

Either we will condition our hearts and minds according to what we think, see, and feel at the human level, or we will allow the Holy Spirit to condition us. We are formed in His image. Hebrews 11:6 tells us that without faith it is impossible to please God. Praise can flow freely when we have genuine faith.

No matter the circumstances, we should resist the temptation to exclaim, "Oh God, You must not love me. God, this cannot be happening to me. Where are You? Why are You allowing these people to do these things? Do You not care?" To consider these thoughts is walking by sight, not trusting that God's ways are higher, and that the things that happen are for our good and His Glory.

We get ourselves into these kinds of attitudes and fixes when we do not stay in the prayer closet and in the Word.

> Then said Jesus to those Jews which believed on him, If ye continue in my word, then are ye my disciples indeed (John 8:31).

We make a daily choice, even sometimes a moment-by-moment choice, to either live by sight or by faith. When we are intimate with Him, we believe Him and spend our time thanking Him and remembering the promises of His Word. Sometimes we praise Him and proclaim things in prayer before we even see them fulfilled. That is when praise for who He is fills our hearts! This praise goes beyond ourselves and reaches into the heavens to join our hearts with the angels as they too glorify Him.

Our Personal Praise Testimony

Believe me, I know that sometimes we receive news that knocks the wind out of us. Things and events can cause fear to try to come to our hearts.

My husband learned the power of praise from his mother early on in his life and after facing daunting conditions. One Sunday, while we were serving in California/Nevada as regional evangelism directors, he preached a powerful sermon on praise. Just two short weeks following that message, we were called to the office of a surgeon. Little did we know that we were going to receive words spoken into our lives that would change us forever. As the doctor began to speak, words like cancer, chemo, radiation, hair loss, fight for life, surgery, 20% chance of survival, began to spill out of her mouth.

We sat there in shock on that Halloween evening, the last patients in the office, as the wind was knocked out of us. There was no history of cancer in my family. I was one of eight children and not one of them had ever had cancer, even though some of them had smoked. I had gotten saved when I was just thirteen years old, why would I have cancer? I even said to the doctor as she spoke those words into my life, "Take it all back. I've just had a baby that we have waited to have for over eight years." Then I was told that because I had just given birth, the estrogen that had been released in my body would cause the cancer to spread. Prior to that moment, we had been celebrating our newborn feeling so blessed, as it had been prophesied that we would have another child. "God, will You now allow me to die from cancer?" I would be lying to you if I told you those thoughts did not come to torment my mind.

My husband and I walked out of the office feeling as empty and lonely as our van looked in the huge, empty parking lot. We could not, dared not even speak a word of what had just been spoken into our lives. We wrestled in our own hearts and minds with fear, about perhaps losing our dreams of growing old and raising our children together. All of these things were going through our minds.

As my husband went in to purchase the prescription that was needed prior to surgery, the very first music he heard after my "death sentence," was a song playing over the drug store intercom that said, "you should have told them you loved them while they were alive." Still in shock, he felt as if he were living in someone else's nightmare.

Both he and I had learned the power of spoken words. We knew we had come under an attack of death, disease, and disappointments. We dared not repeat our evil reports to anyone until we took them to the Lord.

Everyone has their own way of praying, including my husband and me. He paces and prays while I get in my little corner and bury my face in pillows or my hands. We went to our respective areas of prayer. *It is important to have those areas in your home and to go there every day.* We began to call on the Name of the Lord. We told Him what the doctor had said to us. *Yes, we know He already knew, however, prayer is talking things out with our Heavenly Father.* We poured out our hearts and fears to God.

As my husband and I came back together, we confirmed that we had heard the same thing from the Lord: this cancer did not take Him by surprise. Aren't you glad He is never surprised! He was still a good God. His Word did not change because of the words of the doctor, in that He had plans for us that were for our good and not for evil (Jeremiah 29:11). We remembered that

Jesus had, in fact, already taken the stripes that were so needed in my life for healing (Isaiah 53:5). Our provision was already there. *We knew our lives had to testify of these things through our praise to the Lord for who He is even though we faced things that we did not understand.*

It was because of our great love, faith, and trust in the Lord that we wanted to glorify Him no matter what! As children of God, His Word says that He orders our steps. We don't want to grieve Him by not trusting Him when we don't understand where those steps will take us. After taking our report to the Lord and getting His battle plan, we called a few close friends and family members. As we shared the news, we also asked them to join us in praising the Lord and trusting Him for His will throughout this new path we had just been forced to follow.

Remember how just a few short weeks prior to this evil report in our lives, my husband had preached on praise? Well, now we knew that God had given him that sermon for us too. The message was taken from 2 Chronicles 20. As we discuss this chapter, you will see how we put it into practice. His Word became the life-giving stepping stones to enable us to walk with Him day by day in praise-filled prayer.

The Position of our Prayer of Praise—Is When We Seek the Lord

Let's look at 2 Chronicles 20. After Jehoshaphat received word of three armies, "a great multitude" (vv.

1-2), coming against Him, we are told in verse 3 that Jehoshaphat feared. Who wouldn't fear? Perhaps even today, you have received news that causes your heart to be afraid. Maybe you are battling against tormenting thoughts of some disease you inherited or sin with which you struggle. Note that immediately after Jehoshaphat received this word, he took the position of praise. Verses 3-4 go on to say that after his initial fear, Jehoshaphat "set himself to seek the Lord, and proclaimed a fast throughout all Judah. And Judah gathered themselves together, to ask *help* of the Lord: even out of all the cities of Judah they came to seek the Lord." *The position of praise is to set ourselves up to seek the Lord.*

We learn this position of praise by letting it become a way of life for us. We seek the Lord early in the morning, all through the day, and then in the night hour. It is like learning to breathe. When a baby is being carried in the mother, its lungs are not yet expanded to breathe. It is living in an atmosphere of its own body eliminations, with a hole in its heart in which these fluids enter. However, as this child is pressed through the birth canal, the pressure causes the hole to close and the baby to breathe its first breath.

That is how life is as sinners. We are living in our own stench and eliminations from ourselves and this sinful world, and we have a hole in our heart. Then, as we are born into the Body of Christ, we breathe in the presence of Jesus as our Lord, through the prayer of repentance and salvation. The Lord, in an amazing act of forgiveness and redemption, closes that hole in our heart. Praise, love, and an overwhelming sense of joy fill our lives. As we breathe in the presence of the Lord, our lungs expand like a newborn's, and we have the ability and desire to praise Him. We keep our lungs inflated by reading His Word, praying, and worshipping Him.

Some people live off of oxygen tanks—they could represent people who live off of other people's prayers. Praise the Lord that the breath He gives never runs out, is promised never to leave us or forsake us, and has been freely given. If you are in a struggle even now, go back to the One who died for you, who loves you, and has given His life so that you might have life. Just breathe!

A true disciple must realize that he or she has to have intimacy, belief, trust, thanks, and love for the Father that brings praise into their prayer life, just as we must have air to breathe. These virtues come to us through His Word and praying. It's like inhaling and exhaling; we breathe in His Word and breathe out His Word in prayer and praise.

While sitting in a prayer conference recently and just saying, "Holy Heavenly Father," my heart and body were filled with peace and the presence of the Lord. Try it now, *Holy Heavenly Father*! When God created the heavens and the earth, He breathed, and when we speak we breathe. The power of the words that we breathe into the atmosphere will either come from being in His Spirit, the flesh—or even worse, they may come from Satan himself.

Be careful what you breathe into the lives of those around you. Make it a practice to weigh your words. Do they come from your own flesh, or are they weighed in the presence of God? That is the life of a disciple of Christ—having self-control.

The Proclamation of our Prayer of Praise—
Reminds Others of His Promises

In 2 Chronicles 20:6-13, we see Jehoshaphat as he stands before all of the people and their children. *Our children are watching to see how we react to bad news.* Jehoshaphat began to proclaim who God was and tell of His promises to them. He told God of their situation, and proclaimed that even though these armies were against them, their eyes were upon the Lord and not their circumstances! After proclaiming his praise, Jehoshaphat heard the Word of God through the prophet Jahaziel (v. 14).

Notice that when Jehoshaphat positioned himself and proclaimed His faith in God by remembering His promises, God sent His Word. "Then . . . came the Spirit of the Lord in the midst of the congregation" (v. 14). Praise the Lord! They all witnessed the Spirit of the Lord, even the children. The Lord said to them exactly what He is saying to us today when our fears encompass us. " . . . Be not afraid nor dismayed by reason of this great multitude; for the battle is not yours, but God's" (v. 15). The Lord further says, "Ye shall not need to fight in this battle; set yourselves, stand ye still, and see the salvation of the Lord with you, Oh Judah and Jerusalem: fear not, nor be dismayed; tomorrow go out against them; for the Lord will be with you" (v. 17).

With the three armies still threatening to kill them, "Jehoshaphat stood and said, Hear me, Oh Judah, and ye inhabitants of Jerusalem; Believe in the Lord your God, so shall ye be established; believe his prophets, so shall ye prosper" (v. 20). Thank the Lord for those that will continue to stand. The only thing that had changed here is that the people had taken their fears to the Lord and prayerfully called upon Him for help. *In fact, they reminded the Lord of His promises to them.* When the prophet spoke (v. 15), he called them Judah and Jerusalem. As children, when we got into trouble, sometimes our parents would call us our entire name. They were reminding us of who we were, whose we were, and how they expected us to act. These were people of Judah (praise) and Jerusalem (peace). Sometimes we need to be reminded who we are, to whom we belong, and how we are required to act. After all, we are the children of God.

The Purposes of our Prayer of Praise

To Worship The Lord and To Lead Others to Worship Him

When we take the prayer position of praise and begin to speak forth its proclamations, we then see the purpose of praise. Look in 2 Chronicles 20:18. "And Jehoshaphat bowed *his* head with his face to the ground: and all Judah and the inhabitants of Jerusalem fell before the Lord, worshipping the Lord."

Do you see? Fear came knocking, just like it did for my husband and me on that Halloween night in 2000. Fear came to us in the form of words from an authority figure. We appreciated all of her years of study and knowledge; she was a good doctor and called things as she saw them to be (her truth). However, disciples do not walk by sight. As children of God, we walk by faith, *the real truth.* This kind of faith comes after you have positioned yourself in praise by reading His Word, proclaiming His promises, and believing even before you see His hand at work.

Closely examine what happens in verse 18. Even before the battle was won, Jehoshaphat, Judah, and the inhabitants of Jerusalem all worshipped and praised the Lord! This is preemptive praise that we send to our Father before we see His deliverance. We praise the Lord because of who He is, because of His promises to us, and because we love and trust Him. When we have a relationship with God already and have hidden His Word in our hearts, we find breathing easier when fear comes knocking on our doors. We remember whose we are and that nothing comes to us except that which the Lord allows.

My husband and I worshipped and praised the Lord so much during our walk through cancer. Our infant son, at just around six months old, would raise His hands when we would start talking to someone about our trust in God and how we were praising Him. Our oldest son, who was

11 years old, had just attended the funeral of a classmate's mother who died from the same cancer. When we went to tell him that we had been told I had cancer, his answer to us was, "That's okay. I figured something was up. So I went to the Lord and He told me that everything was going to be all right."

On one occasion, I was rushed to the hospital as a result of an allergic reaction to the anti-nausea medication. Fear came to us all as I struggled to breathe. Our son, feeling that panic and anxiety, found a place to pray in the restroom at the hospital. When our state overseer found him at the hospital, with tears running down his face, our 11-year-old son said, "I'm okay. I went to the Lord, and he said everything was going to be okay."

It is important for us as parents, leaders, and Christians, to show our children and all of our "Judah and the inhabitants of Jerusalem" that we take our fears to the Lord, that we remember His promises, and that we praise Him even before our eyes see God's deliverance! When we show them the way, when fear comes knocking on their hearts, they will then know to take their own fears to the Lord just as they have been taught. Jesus modeled this after Lazarus died when he said,

> Jesus saith unto her, Said I not unto thee, that, if thou wouldest believe, thou shouldest see the glory of God? Then they took away the stone from the place where the dead was laid. And Jesus lifted up his eyes, and said, Father, I thank thee that thou

hast heard me. And I knew that thou hearest me always: but because of the people which stand by I said it, that they may believe that thou hast sent me (John 11:40-42).

Jesus, for the purpose of praise and worship to the Father, prayed with faith and preemptive praise, while Lazarus was still quite dead. He prayed so that we, His children, would believe too. He was teaching us just like He wants us to teach our children and those that don't yet believe upon Him. The world, the church, and our families are all looking for those whom the Father has sent. They are looking for those that will believe God is worthy of praise and that He answers His disciples' prayers before they see Lazarus raised from the dead— before they see the mountain moved, before they see cancer healed, before they see lost loved ones saved. Our faith-based, praise-powered prayer will always conquer the spirit of hopelessness.

According to the numbers of the armies that came against Jehoshaphat, God's people should have been killed. According to the rules of death, Lazarus should not have been resurrected. According to the statistics, someone with advanced cancer should not live but die. Thank the Lord that we are never limited to what we see, think, feel, or anything else. We are children of the Lord God Almighty, who can do exceedingly above anything we can comprehend. He hung the stars in the sky and named them all. He spoke this world into existence. No matter what you are facing, pray the prayer of praise to God and see Him work all things together for your good and His glory. When we become His children, we receive the healing blood of Jesus over all of our diseases and the inheritance that He has provided for us.

<u>To Confuse the Enemy</u>

Satan wants to steal our praise, our hope, our peace, and our future. He wants us to doubt God's Word and doubt that God loves us. When we proclaim His promises and continue to prayerfully praise Him, it confuses the enemy. Can you even imagine what the three armies must have thought in verse 21? Jehoshaphat appointed singers unto the Lord and told them that they should, "praise the beauty of holiness, as they went out before the army, and say, Praise the Lord; for his mercy *endureth* forever." They were probably not expecting to see a choir come out to fight them. What must the armies have thought when God's children were already praising the Lord instead of being fearful and cowering back! That would look silly to most. Sometimes, the things the Lord desires of us may seem silly to others. However, if we will follow the example here in 2 Chronicles 20, we will learn the power of praise-filled prayer!

One night I sat on the bathroom floor by the toilet after my fourth or fifth chemo treatment (I was allergic to the anti-nausea medication). I had been so sick that I honestly felt that to die would have been a good thing. I had no control over anything in my body. All of my hair was gone, I felt like death, looked like death, and even smelled of death. I looked at my husband, who was holding my head up with one hand and our baby in his other arm, then I looked at our 11-year-old son as he stood in the bathroom door watching the whole scene.

Right there, that night, I remembered the words of Jahaziel, "Thus saith the Lord unto you, Be not afraid nor dismayed by reason of this great multitude; for the battle is not yours, but God's" (v. 15). "Ye shall not need to fight in this battle: set yourselves, stand ye still, and see the salvation of the Lord with you … fear not, nor be dismayed . . . the Lord *will be* with you" (v. 17). The Word of God caused me to turn to my husband (who I knew was tired as he cared for our children by himself and was no doubt fighting his own battles as he saw what cancer did to me) and to my children. I wanted them to see that I would praise the Lord at all times. I wanted them to see the glory of God, not a dying wife and mother. I didn't even know what that would look like, but His breath through His Word, filled my heart with love for the Lord, my Savior, healer, and deliverer! I turned to my husband, barely able to catch my breath between uncontrollable vomiting and asked him, "Honey, will you praise the Lord for me?"

The presence of the Holy Spirit came into that bathroom as he began to call God every name in the Book . . . "King of Kings, Lord of Lords, Lily of the Valley." The very atmosphere changed, and where death and disease had been, life and healing came into the bathroom as it was filled with praise! My husband continued to pace the floor and in prayer, call out praises to God. Sometimes he would even lay across my sick body and continue with praise to the Lord. Thank the Lord for those that will stand with us through the storms of life and praise the Lord with and for us.

A prayer chain was started where people I did not even know were praying for my healing on a daily basis. Prayer to our holy, loving Heavenly Father with thanksgiving and praise changes the atmosphere. Miracles take place when we disconnect ourselves from artificial oxygen and reconnect with that life-giving breath of the Holy Spirit. Thank You my Lord and my Healer! I love Him so very much!

To Bring the Victory

Look at what happens in 2 Chronicles 20:22: "And when they began to sing and to praise, the Lord set ambushments against the children of Ammon, Moab, and mount Seir, which were come against Judah; and they were smitten." *They didn't wait to sing and praise the Lord after the Lord sent the ambushments. They were already praising the Lord while their lives were still in mortal danger.* This praise comes when we take the position ourselves of seeking His face and praying the prayer of praise, remembering that the purpose of praise is to adore Him and to glorify His Name at all times and in all things! When we glorify Him others will see Him and be saved.

I believe with all of my heart that on that night, in that bathroom, in our Church of God parsonage, death went out the door and the breath of His Word through praise brought life back into my body. As my husband continued for over an hour to call out the Names of the Lord, His Name brought peace, rest, healing, hope, love, and the glory of the Lord into my body, heart, soul, and mind. Oftentimes I've thought, would I have died that night if I had given in to how I looked and felt? I think I might have if I had not looked into the faces of my husband and our children and received His Word at my desperate time. That is when the Holy Spirit prompted me that I could not let them see defeat on my face. I remembered that I was a child of God; I needed to act like it. I would not bow down to any other gods. I would live and die praising my good Lord because I loved Him and trusted Him. I wanted my children and husband to love and trust Him too!

Our perspective changes, when our praying is filled with praise. We understand that it is not up to us after all, for we do not have the power to kill cancer. It was Jesus who took the stripes upon His back for all of our diseases. Oh, what a price He paid for our sins, what great love He has for us even while we were still sinners. Prayer full of praise brings the victory!

About four years ago, our oldest son shared our story while preaching. A rugged, grown man sitting in the back of a small church, broken and without hope, heard him preach from these Scriptures and share the testimony from our lives. This man began to weep, and the power of the Holy Spirit moved deeply upon him. Every opportunity my husband and I are given to tell the story, we see the Living Word of God bring hope, salvation, and healing—even call young and old men and women to trust Him as they begin their ministry.

The Provision of Praise

2 Chronicles 20:20 tells us that they, "went forth into the wilderness of Tekoa; and as they went forth," Jehoshaphat led them in praise. Let's face it, we all go through our times of wilderness, when it looks like everything and everyone in the world is against us. We choose what our response will be during these difficult times. No doubt, I could have pulled lots of sympathies. I could have just wallowed in self-pity and could have gotten angry at God for allowing this cancer in my life. Satan even wanted me to accuse God of not loving me and of leaving me.

When you are daily in the Word of God, and you read story after story of His great love, His kindness, His mercy, and His tenderness toward His children, you learn to trust that He uses these difficult circumstances to bring abundant blessings in our lives. Each time I went for another surgery, test, or treatment—no matter how I felt—I went in and came out praising the Lord.

We asked everyone to pray that our infant son wouldn't be afraid of me when I lost all of my hair. On Christmas

Eve, my sister-in-law shaved the little bit of hair I had left. When he saw me, this 11 month old crawled on top of my head, kissed it, and wrapped his body around my head. That is a provision of praising Him!

Each time I went for another procedure, I would ask God to heal me miraculously, though when He didn't do it the way I asked, I didn't doubt that He was able. Sometimes I felt Him and sometimes I didn't. However, I knew His Word said He would never leave me nor forsake me.

Don't fear Satan and his devices, God even uses him as a delivery man of blessings for His people.

> And when Jehoshaphat and his people came to take away the spoil of them, they found among them in abundance both riches with the dead bodies, and precious jewels, which they stripped off for themselves, more than they could carry away: and they were three days in gathering of the spoil, it was so much. And on the fourth day they assembled themselves in the valley of Berachah; for there they blessed the Lord; therefore the name of the same place was called, The valley of Berachah, unto this day (2 Chronicles 20:25-26).

So this valley in their lives looked like a place of death, loss, and hopelessness. Instead, it became a place of blessings that were too many for them to carry. See, when the enemy comes, he plans to set up house in the places where he wins the victory, therefore he brings in all of his riches. Nevertheless, if we will position ourselves, proclaim His Word, praise God, and understand the purpose of praise is not just for our victory but for those around us, and for His divine glory; we will receive with the provision that praise brings into our lives!

It has been many years since the day that a person of authority and experience spoke words of death into our lives. I can tell you that this place that looked like death has become a place of blessing. My entire family and friends are still enjoying and gathering the blessings it left behind as we tell others of the marvelous works of our living God. We are still praising the Lord and thanking Him. What a mighty God we serve! We love to testify of His goodness, His healing, and His great love, and see the breath of God breathe healing, salvation, hope, and overcoming victory into the lives of others. The glory of the Lord is brought down each time we tell of His goodness. Lives are changed when His glory comes.

The breath of praise brings life into dead, hopeless situations. The Word is alive and powerful. One day, years later, I turned to my husband as we traveled to minister and said, "If I had to go through cancer again to understand what I now know about God, I would do it again." When we learn who God is and to trust Him, we then understand counting it all joy in our sufferings because He is working things for our good and His glory. This heavenly truth will energize your prayer life with praise, victory, and authority. As you pray and share His love with others who are hurting and struggling, you will enter into a pure worship that blesses our Lord and Savior.

SESSION FOUR

My Prayers to Pray

Jehovah-Rophe You are my Healer! You alone have borne my griefs, and You alone have carried my sorrows. Your precious body was pierced for my transgressions. You, Lord Jesus, who had no sin, took stripes upon Your back for all of my diseases. You did this for me while I was yet a sinner and have now freely given this healing to me out of Your great love. I bless Your Name Jehovah-Rophe! I praise You for who You are!

Father God who spoke this world into existence, I praise Your Holy Name! You are the Alpha and Omega; there is no other god like You! You are Jehovah-Jireh, my Provider. You see everything before, in the now, and forevermore. Everything that I could ever need, hope for, or desire is in You! You have provided me with Your love, forgiveness, mercy, wisdom, healing, and peace, and have called me Your own. You sent Your only Son into this world that I might live through Him. You are full of grace and compassion. You have rescued me from death, dried my tears and brought life, health, and strength back to me. You are my Savior, my Healer, and my Deliverer, and I love You Lord. I will forevermore praise Your Holy Name.

I praise You Jehovah-Shalom for the peace that only You can bring to my life, my family, and my church! In this world full of trouble and grief, I can run to You and receive perfect peace and perfect love. Thank You God for Your peace. I praise You for the peace that You bring to our home, to work, to our church, and to the families that are struggling right now. Lord, Your peace passes all understanding. Even though I don't understand why things have turned out the way they have, I know that You order my steps. Knowing that You are the One that is working all things in my life and the lives of those that I know and love brings peace to my heart. Thank You Lord! I praise You Prince of Peace!

SESSION FOUR

Questions for Discussion and Reflection

1. When fear comes knocking at your door, what do you do first? Do you take the position of praise by first seeking the Lord in prayer, or do you first look to tell someone in hopes of receiving sympathy?

2. Do you have faith in God as you go through your own struggles? Why not? Have you gone to the tree of knowledge of good and evil and taken the fruit from that tree? Have you continued to walk in a relationship with Jesus trusting His Word?

3. How much time do you spend in prayer sincerely praising the Lord because you love Him and trust Him? Do you proclaim His promises for your life and the lives of those for whom you pray? How much time do you spend telling God about your doubts, problems, or struggles?

4. Do you realize the purpose of praise? What is going on in your life right now where you can confuse the enemy and praise God for His promises? Who else in

your family and church can you get to praise the Lord with you so their faith can grow too?

5. Do you have a personal prayer of praise testimony that could be passed down through your children and grandchildren? Do you continue to tell them how praising the Lord changed the course of the events of your life?

6. What blessings has praise brought into your life, the lives of other family members, or into your church? How can you and your church remember those blessings so your children and grandchildren will remember them too?

SESSION FOUR

My Prayer Journal

Praying, The *Breath* of Life

Praying
Is *Spiritual Warfare*

DR. O. WAYNE BREWER

Praying, The *Breath* of Life

SESSION FIVE

Scriptures

Genesis 3:15

And I will put enmity between thee and the woman, and between thy seed and her seed; it shall bruise thy head, and thou shalt bruise his heel.

Isaiah 14:12-15

How art thou fallen from heaven, O Lucifer, son of the morning! how art thou cut down to the ground, which didst weaken the nations!

For thou hast said in thine heart, I will ascend into heaven, I will exalt my throne above the stars of God: I will sit also upon the mount of the congregation, in the sides of the north:

I will ascend above the heights of the clouds; I will be like the most High.

Yet thou shalt be brought down to hell, to the sides of the pit.

Isaiah 54:17

No weapon that is formed against thee shall prosper; and every tongue that shall rise against thee in judgment thou shalt condemn. This is the heritage of the servants of the Lord, and their righteousness is of me, saith the Lord.

Daniel 10:11-14

And he said unto me, O Daniel, a man greatly beloved, understand the words that I speak unto thee, and stand upright: for unto thee am I now sent. And when he had spoken this word unto me, I stood trembling.

Then said he unto me, Fear not, Daniel: for from the first day that thou didst set thine heart to understand, and to chasten thyself before thy God, thy words were heard, and I am come for thy words.

But the prince of the kingdom of Persia withstood me one and twenty days: but, lo, Michael, one of the chief princes, came to help me; and I remained there with the kings of Persia.

Now I am come to make thee understand what shall befall thy people in the latter days: for yet the vision is for many days.

Daniel 10:19-20

And said, O man greatly beloved, fear not: peace be unto thee, be strong, yea, be strong. And when he had spoken unto me, I was strengthened, and said, Let my lord speak; for thou hast strengthened me.

Then said he, Knowest thou wherefore I come unto thee? and now will I return to fight with the prince of Persia:

and when I am gone forth, lo, the prince of Grecia shall come.

Mark 13:34
For the Son of Man is as a man taking a far journey, who left his house, and gave authority to his servants, and to every man his work, and commanded the porter to watch.

Luke 10:17-20
And the seventy returned again with joy, saying, Lord, even the devils are subject unto us through thy name.

And he said unto them, I beheld Satan as lightning fall from heaven.

Behold, I give unto you power to tread on serpents and scorpions, and over all the power of the enemy: and nothing shall by any means hurt you.

Notwithstanding in this rejoice not, that the spirits are subject unto you; but rather rejoice, because your names are written in heaven.

Ephesians 6:11-12
Put on the whole armour of God, that ye may be able to stand against the wiles of the devil.

For we wrestle not against flesh and blood, but against principalities, against powers, against the rulers of the darkness of this world, against spiritual wickedness in high places.

James 4:7-8
Submit yourselves therefore to God. Resist the devil, and he will flee from you.

Draw nigh to God, and he will draw nigh to you. Cleanse *your* hands, *ye* sinners; and purify *your* hearts, *ye* double minded.

1 Peter 5:8
Be sober, be vigilant; because your adversary the devil, as a roaring lion, walketh about, seeking whom he may devour.

Study

THINK ABOUT IT. WE ARE AT WAR! Praying is knowing, believing, thanking, and praising God—but praying is also spiritual warfare. Being a disciple of Jesus Christ entails the responsibility of being a prayer warrior.

Prayer Warriors Have Three Enemies

Carrying out prayerful spiritual warfare brings three enemies to the prayer warrior. Scripture gives ample support to this fact.

The World is Our Enemy

Our first enemy is the world. This sin-cursed, fallen world presents to those who seek to live for God a difficult, but not insurmountable, wall of opposition. The world is clearly placed in category of enemy when we are told that our love for the world proves "the love of the Father is not in [us]" (1 John 2:15). The world is the sin-distorted social environment of customs, assumptions, idols, attitudes, and influences in which we all live. John 15:18 tells us that the world hated Jesus even before it hated us. Praise God though, because we overcome. 1 John 5:5 tells us that the one who overcomes the world is the one who believes that Jesus is the Son of God. Aren't you glad that

Jesus prayed to the Father for us, in John 17:15, so that we would be kept from the evil in the world?

The Flesh is Our Enemy

Our second enemy is our own sinful nature. The Word refers to this nature as the flesh. More persistent than any evil spirit, the flesh must be fought. Fighting our flesh is like fighting a civil war on the inside. Galatians 5:17 declares that "the flesh lusteth against the Spirit, and the Spirit against the flesh . . ." Our flesh nature is rightly termed the enemy within. The flesh is our inner inclination to commit sin and is a direct product of the fall of Adam and Eve in the Garden of Eden when they were deceived by the serpent and doubted God.

The downward pull of the flesh is like the force of gravity on the earth. Nevertheless, birds, bees, and jet airliners still fly and go where they want to go because God makes a way. You are always subject to sin, but you do not have to sin if you are a believer and walk in the Spirit of God (See Romans 7:4-6; 8:1-7; Galatians 5:16, 17, 24, 25; and Colossians 3:1-5).

The Devil is Our Enemy

Our third enemy is Satan and his dark kingdom. Today, many in the Christian world are reluctant to speak, much less teach, about the reality and power of Satan. Jesus, however, had no such qualms. More than anyone else in the entirety of Scripture, our Lord taught us about our supernatural adversary. In turn, His disciples taught the early church who Satan was, how he worked, and how the children of God could defeat his devices. Peter squarely referred to Satan as "your adversary the devil" in 1 Peter 5:8. We cannot ignore that in the New Testament alone there are 120 references to Satan and 208 references to evil spirits!

Satan is after all the origin of sin in the universe. Satan, it should be remembered, is far from being all-powerful. According to Colossians 2:15, Jesus made an open show of triumph over the dark kingdom of the devil. Jesus witnessed his fall from heaven and then defeated him on earth. Further, He has given us, His Spirit-filled disciples, authority over the enemy and his kingdom. This eye opening incident is recorded for us in Luke 10:

> And the seventy returned again with joy, saying, Lord, even the devils are subject unto us through thy name. And he said unto them, I beheld Satan as lightning fall from heaven. Behold, I give unto you power to tread on serpents and scorpions, and over all the power of the enemy: and nothing shall by any means hurt you. Notwithstanding in this rejoice not, that the spirits are subject unto you; but rather rejoice, because your names are written in heaven (vv. 17-20).

His Nature is Adversarial

Satan, our adversary, is the "accuser of the brethren" (Revelation 12:10); Apollyon, or "destroyer" (Revelation 9:11); the "god of this world" (2 Corinthians 4:4); the "prince of the power of the air" (Ephesians 2:2); and a "liar" (John 8:44). While God is for us and Jesus died for us, Satan is the constant enemy of Christians and indeed, every living human being. Simply studying the names and titles given to him in Scripture gives a clear insight into the adversarial natural of Satan. Ultimately, his purpose is one of opposition, accusation, seduction, deception, and destruction.

His Kingdom is Real

Ephesians 6:12 warns us, "For we wrestle not against flesh and blood, but against principalities, against powers, against the rulers of the darkness of this world, against spiritual wickedness in high places." Your enemy is not a person. Your enemies are demonic.

Who and what are these different categories of demons? There is a demonic hierarchy under the dominion of Satan who wage war against the Kingdom of God all over the earth and heavens. The principalities (*Archai*) of Ephesians 6:12 appear to be territorial demonic spirits who exercise influence in a particular geographical area. The powers (*Exousiai*), according to Francis Frangipane[3], work in subjection to a principality, and have as their primary activity the task of blanketing "a given area with the energy of its particular evil," for example, the powers of *fear*, *depression*, or *violence*. The "rulers of darkness of this world" (*Kosmokratores*) appear to be a particular class of principality which exert an evil influence on a national scale, not unlike the *Prince over Persia* mentioned in Daniel 10. While there are differing opinions, it is not entirely clear if the "spiritual wickedness in high places" (*Pneumatika*), is another separate hierarchical class of demons, and if so, what exactly they are meant to be. The important point is that the New Testament teaches clearly that Jesus triumphed over them all and Christians now walk in Christ's authority.

Daniel: Case Study of a Prayer Warrior

Being a prayer warrior isn't easy but it does carry certain rewards. One reward is being a partner with God in carrying out His will. Another reward is that the Lord sometimes speaks to prayer warriors in dramatic ways. One such biblical incident is recorded in Daniel 10.

What Kind of Man was Daniel?

Daniel was a man who loved God and was both fearless and persistent in his devotion to the Almighty. These qualities were most clearly exhibited in his prayer life. He was an intercessor for God's people and prayer warrior for God's purpose. He was renowned for his personal prayer life.

---

3   Frangipane, *The Three Battlegrounds*, 149

Both of my grandmothers were like Daniel. My father's mother knew how to pray, prophesied (even the death of President Kennedy and my own coming ministry—at the time of my birth), and cast out devils. My mother's mother was more like the widow Anna (Luke 2:37) who spent hours every day in prayer, half of which would be praying in tongues (as we heard her down the hall). O God, raise up a new generation of prayer warriors like Daniel!

Daniel's reputation for kneeling and praying three times a day is what eventually brought him into contact with the enemy. Daniel's enemies heard him praying. Daniel 6:11 says, "Then these men assembled, and found Daniel praying and making supplication before his God." These men then persuaded the Persian King Darius to sign a decree that no one could petition to any god or man except Darius for 30 days. Naturally, Daniel refused and was thrown into the lion's den. God, however, shut the lion's mouth, and King Darius then threw Daniel's accusers and their families into the same den of lions. God did not shut the lion's mouths this time. Daniel, the prayer warrior, was vindicated and God was glorified.

What Spiritual Warfare was Encountered?

Daniel 10 is a fascinating account which exhibits just how powerful a prayer warrior he was! He was so persistent in his love for God and God's purposes that he prayed beyond the limitations of his flesh and the smaller demonic-imps of hell that most of us encounter. He brought the holy angelic power of God to bear against a demonic *ruler of darkness* or *principality* (that Paul speaks of in Ephesians 6:12).

When the messenger of the Lord appeared to Daniel, he reported that he had been delayed for 21 days by an arch-demon, that he referred to as the *Prince of Persia*. However, God eventually sent the Archangel Michael, one of the chief princes, to help him fight the demonic Prince of Persia. A few verses later (in Daniel 10:20), he mentions another angelic being he called the *Prince of Grecia*. This is high-level spiritual warfare indeed! The invisible kingdom of prayer is every bit as real as the world you and I experience every day with our five senses.

What Truths Does Satan Want to Hide from Prayer Warriors?

Satan is a liar. He tried to obscure the truth of God's love and favor from Daniel as we witnessed earlier. As a true prayer warrior, there are some vital bits of spiritual information that the devil does not want you to know, and truths he will omit. Demons will speak to people who are willing to listen, and they lie and make it up as they go along. Holy angels, however, share with disciples only what God tells them to say (*angel* in New Testament Greek simply means *messenger*).

In Daniel 10, Daniel first beheld One whom we know to be the pre-incarnate Christ who had *the appearance of lightning and His eyes as lamps of fire.* Then, it appears that a holy angel spoke to Daniel and told him truths that God obviously wanted to tell this tired prayer warrior. These truths are facts that Satan doesn't want you to know:

1. First, in Daniel 10:12, we know Daniel was experiencing fear because the angel said, "Fear not."

2. Second, we know that he was wondering why his prayers didn't seem to be getting through, because God had an angel to reassure him.

   Then said he unto me, Fear not, Daniel: for from the first day that thou didst set thine heart to understand, and to chasten thyself before thy God, thy words were heard, and I am come for thy words (Daniel 10:12).

3. Third, Daniel, like many of us today wondered if his prayers were effective. The answer to this question was that the angel had come specifically because of Daniel's words (praying).

4. Fourth, Daniel wondered (as we often do), "Why are my prayers taking so long to be answered?" The angel then gave him the insight of the ferocious spiritual warfare that was transpiring in the heavenlies!

5. Fifth, Daniel confessed to having no strength. Do you ever feel weak from spiritual warfare? I think we all do from time to time. In verse 18 Daniel was divinely strengthened.

6. Sixth, Daniel may have been worn down spiritually; he was weak, felt unloved, and was fearful. Again, however, God's messenger twice told Daniel that he was "a man greatly beloved" (vv. 11, 19) and to "fear not" and "be strong." Isn't it wonderful to realize how much our Savior truly loves and cares for His front-line prayer warriors?

Rules of Engagement for Prayer Warriors

<u>Our Battle Plan</u>

In waging a successful prayer warfare against the enemy, the child of God should understand certain rules of engagement. Let's allow James to shed some light for us.

> Submit yourselves therefore to God. Resist the devil, and he will flee from you. Draw nigh to God, and he will draw nigh to you. Cleanse your hands, ye sinners; and purify your hearts, ye double minded (James 4:7-8).

This brief but powerful passage gives us our battle plan. It looks like this: (1) Have spiritual humility, so that you can then (2), submit to God. (3) Then and only then can you resist the devil after which (4) he will flee from you. (5) Draw close to God and then (6) cleanse your hands (what you do). (7) Purify your heart (what you think and feel), and you will begin to experience spiritual maturity and be prepared prayerfully to engage the enemy.

Use the Name of Jesus

There is no greater or more spiritually powerful name in the universe than the Name of Jesus. Demons tremble and become fearful at the Name of Jesus. Mark 1 and Luke 4 tell us of an incident in which unclean spirits, who were possessing a man, knew the Lord and His Name. Luke 4 tells us that these unclean spirits, upon being confronted by the Lord, cried out and said,

> Let us alone; what have we to do with thee, thou Jesus of Nazareth? Art thou come to destroy us? I know thee who thou art; the Holy One of God (v. 34).

Clearly, demonic spirits recognize the supreme authority that has the power to destroy even them! Their trembling fear of Jesus and His Name is both evident and justified in the passage of John 14:14. The Lord Himself said that when we ask anything in His Name, He will do it. In Mark 16:17 Jesus said that believers would drive out demons and speak in new tongues—in His Name!

I well remember encountering in my bedroom a visible demonic entity (the only time in my life thus far), which I immediately knew to be a spirit of fear. I had been in intense spiritual warfare for many weeks and things were beginning to look hopeless. The demonic spirit was awful, dark, appeared to be strong, and had a definite air of confidence that he was coming in for the kill. He had come up out of the pit and began to come slowly toward me. At first, I was fearful. Then it came to me and I boldly said, "In the Name of Jesus" and pointed at him. He immediately fled away!

On another occasion about two years earlier, I was getting in some crucial studying time while at home. Unfortunately, that same morning one of our children had a very high, burning fever. I realized Satan was trying to hinder me by striking at my child. Pam had to work and could not be home that day. I went into my sleeping child's bedroom and laid hands on my little one and prayed "In the Name of Jesus, I command you spirit of infirmity to leave this child and take this fever with you!" Two hours later, while I was studying, I heard the pat, pat, pat of little feet and there was my child. I felt his forehead —no fever whatsoever! Then he said, "I had a dream." I said, "Really? Tell me about it." He replied, "Well, I saw Jesus and He put His hand on my head and healed me." *Spiritual warfare requires prayer that takes authority in the Name of Jesus!*

The Prayer of Agreement

If prayer warriors are to be a genuine army working together, serving together and making spiritual war upon the kingdom of Hell, then it must be a unified force under the command of Jesus Christ. *There can be no place for division, strife, and rebellious attitudes. The enemy thrives on such a carnal atmosphere.* The world will not know we are disciples of Christ unless we truly love one another and live out one, unified testimony of loving compassion and purity before a strife-ridden world.

In Acts 2, the world did not comprehend what was going on in the upper room, but the writer of Acts understood full well that the Holy Spirit had come upon a group of believers who were "in one accord." The prayers of agreement between Christians, as well as church-wide corporate prayer, have been hallmarks of the Pentecostal church through the years. There is power in prayer, but there is extra power in the prayer of agreement. When, in Philippians 4:2, Paul speaks of Euodias and Syntyche, he asks them to be "of the same mind." The Holy Spirit seems to be moved by such fervent, unified petition. The agreement and unity of believers are important to the Lord of the church. Just as the Father, the Word, and the Holy Ghost are in unified agreement in heaven, so our Lord prayed that His church would also be one.

> That they may be one; as thou, Father, art in me, and I in thee, that they also may be one in us: that the world may believe that thou hast sent me (John 17:21).

What Fasting Is

Fasting unto the Lord is abstaining from something, normally food, by choice for a given period for the purpose of drawing nearer to God as well as humbling oneself under the Lord. Fasting from food has the effect of weakening the flesh and its dominion over the soul of a person, while at the same time strengthening the spirit. As the *flesh-man* comes under subjection to the spirit-man, one's spiritual senses become sharper, stronger, and more acute. It is a disconnection from the stale breath of the world that in turn allows us to receive once again the breath of the Lord into our lives.

Fasting should be done unto the Lord as a way of softening a callused heart and preparing the *spirit-man* for sincere, effective prayer. Just as a message in tongues and interpretation of tongues are complementary spiritual gifts (in pairing), so fasting complements prayer. Without prayer, in fact, fasting would be a useless, needless ritual.

What Fasting Does

Within the context of prayer warfare, fasting has at least four essential purposes:

1. First, fasting demonstrates and strengthens humility and sorrow over sin. In 1 Samuel 7:1-6, the people fasted and confessed their sins to the Lord. Freedom from sin is a prerequisite for effective warfare.

2. Second, fasting helps to loose those who are oppressed. Isaiah 58:6 talks about the fast that God chooses to set the oppressed free and break yokes of bondage.

3. Third, fasting helps us to get our flesh in a position of submission so that we can clearly receive divine direction from the Lord. It was while the church was worshipping and fasting that the Holy Spirit broke in and gave direction that Saul and Barnabus were to be set apart for missionary work (Acts 13:2).

4. Fourth, fasting and prayer are sometimes necessary to deliver some individuals from demonic control (Matthew 17:21). It is significant that the first action of our Lord after His baptism was to prepare Himself through fasting and prayer. It is clear that genuine, Spirit-led fasting serves as a preparation for prayer-breakthrough. The humbling of the soul and controlling of the flesh through fasting is a component of warfare modeled before us by Jesus Himself.

You may wish to consult with Appendix Four, *Why Fasting*.

A Prayer Warrior is a Persistent Fighter

Are you prayer warrior? A true prayer warrior is a fighter. Every day, every week, every month, a prayer warrior fights the kingdom of Hell on his or her knees. This is exactly how Daniel won his battles even against powerful human and demonic opposition. A prayer warrior *prays* the price of travailing in intercession in order to birth into existence God's will. A prayer warrior stays close to the heartbeat of what God is doing and keeps on praying.

Like the widow that Jesus speaks of in Luke 18, spiritual warfare praying must be determined and persistent. You and I must be like spiritual pit bulls that refuse to let go. Don't let the devil wear you out. You wear him out with your fervent praying.

Praying, The *Breath* of Life

My Prayers to Pray

O Lord, I love You and I don't want there to be anything that rivals my affections and obedience to You. Give me victory over the three enemies of my soul. Please take away my worldly attitudes and appetites. Sanctify me as I crucify my flesh and its desires. Deliver me from the evil one and all of his snares, deceptions, and accusations.

Dear Father, please help me and deliver me and my family from every stronghold of sin that seeks to enslave me, my spouse, or any of our children.

Dear Lord, in Your Name I adhere to 2 Corinthians 10:5 and cast down imaginations and every high thing that exalts itself against the knowledge of God. I bring every thought into captivity to the obedience of Christ.

O God, I commit myself to the daily study of Your Word and to have a special time with You. I submit myself, my time, my desires, and my plans to You and ask You to help me resist the devil, knowing he will flee from me. *Lord* I come into agreement with my brothers and sisters who are here with me right now. We agree, believe, and ask You to send a spirit of love and hunger for You into our church.

Questions for Discussion and Reflection

1. Do I understand that praying to God is a matter of asking in faith, while speaking to the enemy (which should be a minimal activity) is a matter of demanding and taking authority over his devices in Jesus' Name?

2. How often and seriously do I take my responsibility for praying a hedge of protection around my family? Do I pray for the preservation of love, unity, and God's protection over my church?

3. Do I trust and believe in the power of God to work things out according to His desires? Or, do I have preconceived thoughts about what should happen in circumstances involving my family and my church?

4. How often do I pray for spiritual protection around my pastor and his family? Do I pray for divine wisdom and anointing upon him/her to hear God clearly and to have the boldness to act?

5. Have I read James 4:7-8 and am I having a hard time resisting the devil because I have not submitted to God?

6. Do I pray in the Name of Jesus against wicked spirits that seek to control me or others (spirit of pride, spirit of jealousy, spirit of unforgiveness, spirit of fear, spirit of homosexuality, etc.)?

7. Do I pray to God to use me to encourage the body of Christ and resist the satanic temptation to accuse others of wrongdoing? Do I have to be reminded that the Holy Spirit is the Comforter and Satan is called the accuser of the brethren?

SESSION FIVE

My Prayer Journal

Praying, The *Breath* of Life

Praying

Is *Refusing* to Give Up

PAMELA R. BREWER

Praying, The *Breath* of Life

Scriptures

Joshua 1:9

Have not I commanded thee? Be strong and of a good courage; be not afraid, neither be thou dismayed: for the Lord thy God is with thee whithersoever thou goest.

Psalm 18:32

It is God that girdeth me with strength, and maketh my way perfect.

Luke 18:1-8

And he spake a parable unto them to this end, that men ought always to pray, and not to faint;

Saying, There was in a city a judge, which feared not God, neither regarded man:

And there was a widow in that city; and she came unto him, saying, Avenge me of mine adversary.

And he would not for a while: but afterward he said within himself, Though I fear not God, nor regard man; Yet because this widow troubleth me, I will avenge her, lest by her continual coming she weary me.

And the Lord said, Hear what the unjust judge saith.

And shall not God avenge his own elect, which cry day and night unto him, though he bear long with them?

I tell you that he will avenge them speedily. Nevertheless when the Son of man cometh, shall he find faith on the earth?

Ephesians 3:18-19
May be able to comprehend with all saints what is the breadth, and length, and depth, and height;

And to know the love of Christ, which passeth knowledge, that ye might be filled with all the fulness of God.

Philippians 4:12-13
I know both how to be abased, and I know how to abound: every where and in all things I am instructed both to be full and to be hungry, both to abound and to suffer need.

I can do all things through Christ which strengtheneth me.

Hebrews 10:35-36
Cast not away therefore your confidence, which hath great recompense of reward.

For ye have need of patience, that, after ye have done the will of God, ye might receive the promise.

James 1:4-6

But let patience have her perfect work, that ye may be perfect and entire, wanting nothing.

If any of you lack wisdom, let him ask of God, that giveth to all men liberally, and upbraideth not; and it shall be given him.

But let him ask in faith, nothing wavering. For he that wavereth is like a wave of the sea driven with the wind and tossed.

James 5:11

Behold, we count them happy which endure. Ye have heard of the patience of Job, and have seen the end of the Lord; that the Lord is very pitiful, and of tender mercy.

Study

THERE ARE TIMES IN MOST EVERYONE'S life when they feel like giving up. People can disappoint us and leave us broken, doubting, lonely, or confused. Circumstances in life can seem to pull the rug out from under our feet and leave us feeling like giving up. The economy, a business, dreams, finances, children, a spouse, health, and many other things may fail us. There are many reasons a person may feel like giving up.

Maybe as you have read and prayed through this study, you too have found yourself in a struggle. Earlier, we talked about how the heart of a developing baby is formed with a hole in the top and the bottom as it is in the womb. Psalm 139 speaks of how God Himself formed us,

> For You formed my inward parts; You covered me in my mother's womb. I will praise You, for I am fearfully *and* wonderfully made (vv. 13-14 NKJV).

You may remember that as a baby is pressed through the birth canal and takes in the first breath, he is no longer breathing in his own bodily fluids and eliminations. The hole in the heart closes and oxygen from the air begins flowing into the lungs.

When we are born into Christ, all things become new. We are no longer living on the life-support of this earth. We are now in Him; He has created in us a clean heart. It is in Christ that we live, move, and have our being.

So if you have found yourself struggling or gasping for air lately, maybe you have stepped out of living in Him and breathing in His Spirit. The only way we can stay connected to this life-giving, powerful breath is through staying in His living Word and prayer. Keep praying until the answer comes. Hold on to your confidence in God. It will pay off. Patiently and prayerfully do the will of God and you will receive the promise. Hebrews 10 exhorts us:

> Cast not away therefore your confidence, which hath great recompence of reward. For ye have need of patience, that, after ye have done the will of God, ye might receive the promise (vv. 35-36).

The Widow's Warfare

If you have been in a spiritual struggle lately, don't give up! Don't throw in the towel on what you are praying. Refuse to accept it when the devil is telling you no. In other words, refuse to give up! Jesus tells us ". . . men ought always to pray, and not to faint," Luke 18:1. Then He tells us how to refuse to give up with the story of a persistent widow and the unjust judge in the following verses. Luke writes this chapter after he tells of how Jesus warned us of taking up offenses in chapter 17, and that if we have faith the size of a mustard seed we can move mountains. Here is Jesus' story about the widow in Luke 18:

> And he spake a parable unto them to this end, that men ought always to pray, and not to faint; Saying, There was in a city a judge, which feared not God, neither regarded man: And there was a widow in that city; and she came unto him, saying, Avenge me of mine adversary. And he would not for a while: but afterward he said within himself, Though I fear not God, nor regard man; Yet because this widow troubleth me, I will avenge her, lest by her continual coming she weary me. And the Lord said, Hear what the unjust judge saith. And shall not God avenge his own elect, which cry day and night unto him, though he bear long with them? I tell you that he will avenge them speedily. Nevertheless when the Son of man cometh, shall he find faith on the earth? (vv. 1-8).

This widow had been wronged. Scripture doesn't tell us what was done against her; however, we know from the time of the story that a widow had very few rights. She had no husband, no political clout, apparently no real money to speak of, and on top of it all, she was merely a woman living in the world the way it was 2,000 years ago. She lived in a time when the self-righteous Pharisees would pray a common (but offensive) prayer that said, *I thank You God that I am not a Gentile. I thank You that I am not a dog. I thank You God that I am not a woman.*

The odds were against her. She depended upon her family members once her husband had died. There is no mention of this widow having family she could turn to; however, we know that someone had wronged her. Maybe her husband was owed some money before he died and now the person owing the money would not give her what was owed. Maybe it had to do with her home or some other matter. All we know is that she needed justice imposed upon her adversary. There was a struggle going on between justice and an unjust judge. Have you ever been there? Did you fight, continue to pray, or did you just give up?

In Luke 18, Jesus explicitly states that this is a parable about not giving up in prayer. In this parable of the widow's warfare, we see the three principles involved in refusing to give up when we are praying.

The Principle of Helpless Dependence

The difference to keep in mind in this story is that the widow's judge was unjust. We know that we serve a God who is a righteous judge of all who live. Still, God allows us to go through situations where we are the widow—where we are in an uphill prayer battle, and realize that without Jesus' help, we are helpless. We are utterly dependent upon Him! The widow in Luke 18 had no political clout, yet she was still willing to go to the one who could give her what she needed. As Christians, we know that we can go to our Judge and when we delight ourselves in Him (intimacy with God), He promises to give us the desires of our heart.

> Delight thyself also in the Lord: and he shall give thee the desires of thine heart. Commit thy way unto the Lord; trust also in him; and he shall bring it to pass. And he shall bring forth thy righteousness as the light, and thy judgment as the noonday (Psalm 37:4-6).

The widow did not have what she needed. Neither do we have what we need. Everything we need comes from the hand of God. In Luke 18:8, the Lord asks "when the Son of man cometh, shall he find faith on the earth?" It is His desire that we refuse to give up and that we keep our faith in Him. We know that faith comes by hearing the Word of God. We have to stay connected to our lifeline by reading, studying, meditating, and praying the Scriptures when we are alone with Him.

Remember this: when I am at my most helplessly dependent is also when I can be my most hopefully encouraged, because now I am out of the *me* zone and have passed into the *God* zone. If it is going to be, then it is up to God. Since He never fails, I am going to keep on praying.

The Principle of Spiritual Struggle

Jesus' little widow knows she has an adversary who opposes her. She refers to him as her adversary. What is your adversary? Is it fear, lust, unforgiveness, doubt, depression, jealousy, inferiority, shame, or anxiety? Everyone has their own adversary, but our adversary is also a *who*, as well! We have a *someone* who opposes us. In John 10 Jesus says,

> The thief cometh not, but for to steal, and to kill, and to destroy: I am come that they might have life, and that they might have it more abundantly (v. 10).

We are in a spiritual struggle with an enemy who wants to wear us out. When we struggle in prayer, we are strengthening our spiritual endurance as we become more conformed to the image of Christ. James 5:11 declares, "Behold, we count them happy which endure . . . " We must be like the widow and make up our minds that we are going to wear Satan out by continually going to the Father.

The judge in this story was unjust and did not fear God. In Luke 18:5, he nevertheless gave her what she wanted, "'because this widow troubles me I will avenge her, lest by her continual coming she weary me.'" She refused to give up what she knew belonged to her. God wants us to do the same. *Satan has no right to take what and who belongs to you*!

> Have not I commanded thee? Be strong and of a good courage; be not afraid, neither be thou dismayed: for the Lord thy God is with thee whithersoever thou goest (Joshua 1:9).

We are to press prayerfully on to the prize that is before us and not give up.

If you sometimes feel spiritually tired, it is because you have been wrestling in prayer. But others are watching.

> Wherefore seeing we also are compassed about with so great a cloud of witnesses, let us lay aside every weight, and the sin which doth so easily beset us, and let us run with patience the race that is set before us (Hebrews 12:1).

There are sinners and saints watching us, a cloud of witnesses, that are looking to see if we will give up. We should refuse to give up so that others will see our faith and begin to trust in the Lord for themselves. You will become the living word of God to them. The breath of the Holy Spirit will blow into their lives as they see you stand upon His Word in prayer and not give up!

The Principle of Accessing Authority

If you need help and the one you go to cannot help, go to someone who has the authority to do so. The authority that this widow had access to was an unjust judge who was, no doubt, waiting for a bribe. He knew she was a widow and probably did not have the means to give the bribe that he so greedily desired. She needed someone to step up to the plate who could avenge her. It is noteworthy that in Luke 18:3 when the widow asks for the unjust judge to avenge her of her adversary, the Greek word used in this Scripture is *Ekdikeo* (#1556) which means to *vindicate, retaliate, punish*. She was rightfully angry, and she wanted what belonged to her.

When the Lord said, "And shall not God *avenge* His own elect, which cry out day and night unto Him . . . " (v. 7 italics added), the Greek word used by Jesus for avenge is *Poieo* (#4160) which is a much more spiritually promising and robust word. It means not only *avenge* but also *to bring forth, to cast out, to execute, to lighten the ship*. He not only avenges us, but He will also bring forth the things we are praying into existence, cast out what we are praying against, execute His holy plans, and even lighten the load of our overburdened spiritual ship. His avenging us is always superior to our fleshly desire to simply get even. When we refuse to give up in prayer, God is always "a rewarder of them who diligently seek Him," (Hebrews 11:6). He will avenge us when we refuse to give up.

As Christians, our judge is our Heavenly Father and our attorney is Jesus Christ. Our witness for the defense is the Holy Spirit, as we are told that His Spirit will bear witness with our spirit that we are indeed the children of God. Our court is fixed so that we cannot lose, because Jesus Christ has already won all of our cases for us and He has paid the price with His own life. Here is a tip for your prayer life: When you go before the Divine Judge, always bring the Son of the Judge. The Judge always rules in favor of His beloved Son!

How God Taught Me to Never Give Up

The struggles that we go through in life will make us stronger and will give us what we need to continue in our faith. I grew up in a home that was not Christian. However, when I was a born my parents were attending church. My mother's Sunday school class named me, giving me the middle name of Reneé, which means *reborn*. As a young child, I struggled with convulsions until finally it was discovered that I had a brain tumor. The doctors did not expect me to live through the surgery. My oldest brother took me to the grocery store across the street from our house and had a picture taken of me so they would have something by which to remember me.

Even after my parents stopped attending church, they still told the story of how the Lord healed me, and how this precious Sunday school class prayed at the hospital until they saw the miracle of my healing. One hour after having the brain tumor removed, miraculously I sat up on the bed and asked for my mother. I'm told that I walked down the hospital hall between crying doctors and nurses, into the arms of my mother who was with the ladies from the Sunday school class. They were speaking in other tongues and praising the Lord for my healing. That Sunday school of Spirit-filled prayer warriors (some of them widows) refused to give up interceding for me because they knew to whom they were praying.

Thank the Lord that my parents, although unsaved, still told the story of God's healing power and mercy to me as a child. This story of His healing in my life caused me to love Him. I can never remember a time in my life when I did not have a deep love for the Lord!

I gave my heart to the Lord when I was 13 years old. This caused havoc in my home as our weekends were now interrupted. Most weekends we would be at the lake fishing late into the night. Now we had to leave the lake early to get me home so I could go to church.

To say my parents were not happy to give up their late night fishing was an understatement. I caught rides to church from the church van and neighbors. Sometimes my father would take me if he came home from work early enough. Most times my request to go to church was met with, "not until you have cleaned the bathroom." After I cleaned the bathroom until it was sparkling, I would then ask permission to go to church, again only to hear the answer that the bathroom grout needed to be cleaned, or some other item in the bathroom wasn't clean enough. It was a ploy to discourage me and to cause me to give up. It was a struggle as the widow had with the unjust judge.

I just had to get to church where I could worship God, hear about Him, and be around His people. Sometimes I would spend up to five hours cleaning one little bathroom, the whole time prayerfully refusing to give up. As I cleaned the grout with a toothbrush, I would access the authority of the Holy Spirit, sing the songs I learned in church, and pray the Scriptures. The Psalms were a favorite as I cried out with David, "Deliver me from those that persecute me."

God would always make a way for me to go to church. I would arrive there just in time, with the smell of Clorox and Ajax on me and sometimes still crying because of the struggle. I was too embarrassed to tell anyone what was going on at home and I knew that whatever it took, I would keep asking and keep doing whatever was required to be in the House of the Lord.

It wasn't until after both of my parents went to be with the Lord that this story would be told. When they came to the Lord years later, they were so sorry because of their actions. Out of love and respect for both of them, I would not tell the story while they were living. The battle was with Satan, who was trying to keep me from serving the Lord, and he was working through my parents. Our wrestling in prayer is not with flesh and blood, but rather a prayer struggle with spiritual powers and rulers of dark places that are trying to keep you from all that the Lord has for you.

Many years later, while serving in ministry and battling depression brought on by medications that followed cancer treatment, the Lord brought to my memory that bathroom scene of years before. He told me that it was there that He taught me to pray and never to give up. I learned that when I don't meditate on my circumstances, but praise the Lord and trust in Him, He can deliver me.

As I prayed, He became my strength, my joy, and my power to overcome circumstances. What Satan meant for evil was and still is a blessing in my life. With that insight, the Lord led me to a fast and special prayer where He delivered me from depression and even healed me of an allergy from which I hadn't even asked to be healed. God always blesses us above and beyond what we ask! We should rejoice in the fact that the Almighty is also our loving Father.

Knowing that we are hopelessly dependent upon a loving Heavenly Father who desires to bless us, we should never lose faith and we should refuse to give up. Take all of your concerns to the Father in prayer. He will hear you and He will answer you. Keep on knocking, keep on asking, keep on trusting Him, and refuse to give up! Remember, according to Isaiah 40:31, "they that wait upon the Lord shall renew their strength." Psalm 33:6 says, "By the word of the Lord were the heavens made; and all the host of them by the breath of his mouth." God is powerful and is in charge.

> Then said Jesus to them again, Peace be unto you: as my Father hath sent me, even so send I you. And when he had said this, he breathed on them, and saith unto them, Receive ye the Holy Ghost (John 20:21-22).

The Hebrew word used for Spirit is *ruach*, which means *air in motion*. It is the same word used for breath.

The Scriptures are filled with how His Spirit was breathed into us and how His Spirit creates. Let the Holy Spirit breathe into your prayer life.

As we live in this world, we must be breathing in His Holy Spirit through His Word and prayer. Often our times of struggle are times when Satan is trying to disconnect us from God's truth and our time in prayer. Without a doubt, if you will today get back to being so close to God that you feel His breath in your prayer closet, you will see vibrancy restored in your walk with Christ. When we refuse to give up, and we learn to pursue God like this precious widow pursued justice, God will avenge us speedily and reward us for standing strong. He will bring to you more than you expected, because Jesus said, "men ought always to pray and not to faint" (Luke 18:1).

We live in a world full of sin and have not yet been glorified into our spiritual bodies. As a result, we will have struggles that bring spiritual warfare. Most battles are fought and won in the battlefield of the mind. It is by God's design that our minds affect our breathing, which in turn affects our heart. When our minds are upon the Lord instead of our circumstances, the mind of Christ in us will cause us to overcome. His Holy Spirit breathes life and combats the lies of the enemy with the truth that sets us free. Things spoken to us by well-meaning people, or by those that try to attack us, are combated with His Spirit. As disciples of Christ we can breathe that breath of life into friends, the lost, the broken, the body of Christ, and our families. Ezekiel 37 tells us how to breathe life into situations that are dead.

> And when I beheld, lo, the sinews and the flesh came up upon them, and the skin covered them above: but there was no breath in them. Then said he unto me, Prophesy unto the wind, prophesy, son of man, and say to the wind, Thus saith the Lord God; Come from the four winds, O breath, and breathe upon these slain, that they may live (vv. 8-9).

You don't have to give up. The Bible speaks of those who endure to the end. Keep enduring in prayer until the enemy yields. The enemy is opposing you, but God is preparing you for His perfect plan. The victory is for you to claim in the prayer closet! Prepare yourself for spiritual warfare by putting on the whole amour of God (Ephesians 6:10-20) and by being filled with the Holy Spirit.

My Prayers to Pray

My Father, I am tired and weak and my faith is not what I want it to be. Please help me to settle in and meditate upon Hebrews 10:35-39. Help me to hold on to my confidence in You and be patient as I continue to have faith in Your timing and Your perfect plan for my life.

Dear Lord, help me to stay strong in You and in the power of Your might. Like Abraham, who lived by faith, may I please remember to trust You, stop meditating upon my weaknesses and adverse circumstances, and begin today to praise You for who You are and what You have already planned for me.

Lord Jesus, I declare Your Word and confess that it is true for me. "I can do all things through Christ who strengthens me" (Philippians 4:13 NKJV).

Father God, like the widow that Jesus talked about, I appeal to You as my righteous judge, Your Son Jesus as my defense attorney, and the Holy Spirit as my witness. Avenge me of my adversary the devil in this matter in which I am involved.

Dear God, I stand on Isaiah 40:27-31. You give power to the faint and strength to the weak. You will renew my strength as I wait upon You.

Questions for Discussion and Reflection

1. Have I brought the Word of God into my prayer closet and my heart? When I feel like giving up, have I meditated upon Hebrews 10:35-39 which states things like, "don't throw away your confidence," "you have need of patience," "the just shall live by faith," "we are not one of those who draw back"?

2. Do I pray, "Yes Lord, I know that, 'the steps of a good man are ordered by the Lord'" (Psalm 37:23)? Do I believe this Scripture? Do I act and talk as though I believe it?

3. Go back and study the story of the widow and how Jesus said that we should always pray and not give up. Am I truly being persistent in praying and fighting the "widow's warfare"?

4. When I feel like giving up, quitting and throwing in the towel, do I consider that the devil is trying to defeat me? Or, is it a case of my Heavenly Father lovingly disciplining me, stretching my faith, and conforming me to the image of His Son, Christ Jesus?

5. When I'm tempted to give up, do I go into my prayer closet? Or, do I seek to alleviate stress through seeking pleasure, staying on the Internet, overeating, or procrastinating responsibilities?

SESSION SIX
My Prayer Journal

_____

_____

_____

_____

_____

_____

_____

_____

_____

_____

_____

_____

_____

_____

_____

_____

_____

_____

Praying, The *Breath* of Life

Praying

Is *Learning* to Lean

DR. O. WAYNE AND PAMELA R. BREWER

Praying, The *Breath* of Life

SESSION SEVEN

Scriptures

Genesis 32:1-30

And Jacob went on his way, and the angels of God met him.

And when Jacob saw them, he said, This is God's host: and he called the name of that place Mahanaim.

And Jacob sent messengers before him to Esau his brother unto the land of Seir, the country of Edom.

And he commanded them, saying, Thus shall ye speak unto my lord Esau; Thy servant Jacob saith thus, I have sojourned with Laban, and stayed there until now:

And I have oxen, and asses, flocks, and menservants, and womenservants: and I have sent to tell my lord, that I may find grace in thy sight.

And the messengers returned to Jacob, saying, We came to thy brother Esau, and also he cometh to meet thee, and four hundred men with him.

Then Jacob was greatly afraid and distressed: and he divided the people that was with him, and the flocks, and herds, and the camels, into two bands;

And said, If Esau come to the one company, and smite it, then the other company which is left shall escape.

And Jacob said, O God of my father Abraham, and God of my father Isaac, the Lord which saidst unto me, Return unto thy country, and to thy kindred, and I will deal well with thee:

I am not worthy of the least of all the mercies, and of all the truth, which thou hast shewed unto thy servant; for with my staff I passed over this Jordan; and now I am become two bands.

Deliver me, I pray thee, from the hand of my brother, from the hand of Esau: for I fear him, lest he will come and smite me, and the mother with the children.

And thou saidst, I will surely do thee good, and make thy seed as the sand of the sea, which cannot be numbered for multitude.

And he lodged there that same night; and took of that which came to his hand a present for Esau his brother;

Two hundred she goats, and twenty he goats, two hundred ewes, and twenty rams,

Thirty milch camels with their colts, forty kine, and ten bulls, twenty she asses, and ten foals.

And he delivered them into the hand of his servants, every drove by themselves; and said unto his servants, Pass over before me, and put a space betwixt drove and drove.

And he commanded the foremost, saying, When Esau my brother meeteth thee, and asketh thee, saying, Whose art thou? and whither goest thou? and whose are these before thee?

Then thou shalt say, They be thy servant Jacob's; it is a present sent unto my lord Esau: and, behold, also he is behind us.

And so commanded he the second, and the third, and all that followed the droves, saying, On this manner shall ye speak unto Esau, when ye find him.

And say ye moreover, Behold, thy servant Jacob is behind us. For he said, I will appease him with the present that goeth before me, and afterward I will see his face; peradventure he will accept of me.

So went the present over before him: and himself lodged that night in the company.

And he rose up that night, and took his two wives, and his two womenservants, and his eleven sons, and passed over the ford Jabbok.

And he took them, and sent them over the brook, and sent over that he had.

And Jacob was left alone; and there wrestled a man with him until the breaking of the day.

And when he saw that he prevailed not against him, he touched the hollow of his thigh; and the hollow of Jacob's thigh was out of joint, as he wrestled with him.

And he said, Let me go, for the day breaketh. And he said, I will not let thee go, except thou bless me.

And he said unto him, What is thy name? And he said, Jacob.

And he said, Thy name shall be called no more Jacob, but Israel: for as a prince hast thou power with God and with men, and hast prevailed.

And Jacob asked him, and said, Tell me, I pray thee, thy name. And he said, Wherefore is it that thou dost ask after my name? And he blessed him there.

And Jacob called the name of the place Peniel: for I have seen God face to face, and my life is preserved.

1 Samuel 21:10-15
And David arose and fled that day for fear of Saul, and went to Achish the king of Gath.

And the servants of Achish said unto him, Is not this David the king of the land? did they not sing one to another of him in dances, saying, Saul hath slain his thousands, and David his ten thousands?

And David laid up these words in his heart, and was sore afraid of Achish the king of Gath.

And he changed his behaviour before them, and feigned himself mad in their hands, and scrabbled on the doors of the gate, and let his spittle fall down upon his beard.

Then said Achish unto his servants, Lo, ye see the man is mad: wherefore then have ye brought him to me?

Have I need of mad men, that ye have brought this fellow to play the mad man in my presence? shall this fellow come into my house?

Psalm 142:1-7
I cried unto the Lord with my voice; with my voice unto the Lord did I make my supplication.

I poured out my complaint before him; I shewed before him my trouble.

When my spirit was overwhelmed within me, then thou knewest my path. In the way wherein I walked have they privily laid a snare for me.

I looked on my right hand, and beheld, but there was no man that would know me: refuge failed me; no man cared for my soul.

I cried unto thee, O Lord: I said, Thou art my refuge and my portion in the land of the living.

Attend unto my cry; for I am brought very low: deliver me from my persecutors; for they are stronger than I.

Bring my soul out of prison, that I may praise thy name: the righteous shall compass me about; for thou shalt deal bountifully with me.

Psalm 143:1

Hear my prayer, O Lord, give ear to my supplications: in thy faithfulness answer me, and in thy righteousness.

Psalm 146:5

Happy is he that hath the God of Jacob for his help, whose hope is in the Lord his God.

Matthew 11:28-30

Come unto me, all ye that labour and are heavy laden, and I will give you rest.

Take my yoke upon you, and learn of me; for I am meek and lowly in heart: and ye shall find rest unto your souls.

For my yoke is easy, and my burden is light.

Matthew 15:22-28

And, behold, a woman of Canaan came out of the same coasts, and cried unto him, saying, Have mercy on me, O Lord, thou son of David; my daughter is grievously vexed with a devil.

But he answered her not a word. And his disciples came and besought him, saying, Send her away; for she crieth after us.

But he answered and said, I am not sent but unto the lost sheep of the house of Israel.

Then came she and worshipped him, saying, Lord, help me.

But he answered and said, It is not meet to take the children's bread, and to cast it to dogs.

And she said, Truth, Lord: yet the dogs eat of the crumbs which fall from their masters' table.

Then Jesus answered and said unto her, O woman, great is thy faith: be it unto thee even as thou wilt. And her daughter was made whole from that very hour.

Luke 24:13-32

And, behold, two of them went that same day to a village called Emmaus, which was from Jerusalem *about* threescore furlongs.

And they talked together of all these things which had happened.

And it came to pass, that, while they communed *together* and reasoned, Jesus himself drew near, and went with them.

But their eyes were holden that they should not know him.

And he said unto them, What manner of communications *are* these that ye have one to another, as ye walk, and are sad?

And the one of them, whose name was Cleopas, answering said unto him, Art thou only a stranger in Jerusalem, and hast not known the things which are come to pass there in these days?

And he said unto them, What things? And they said unto him, Concerning Jesus of Nazareth, which was a prophet mighty in deed and word before God and all the people:

And how the chief priests and our rulers delivered him to be condemned to death, and have crucified him.

But we trusted that it had been he which should have redeemed Israel: and beside all this, to day is the third day since these things were done.

Yea, and certain women also of our company made us astonished, which were early at the sepulchre;

And when they found not his body, they came, saying, that they had also seen a vision of angels, which said that he was alive.

And certain of them which were with us went to the sepulchre, and found *it* even so as the women had said: but him they saw not.

Then he said unto them, O fools, and slow of heart to believe all that the prophets have spoken:

Ought not Christ to have suffered these things, and to enter into his glory?

And beginning at Moses and all the prophets, he expounded unto them in all the scriptures the things concerning himself.

And they drew nigh unto the village, whither they went: and he made as though he would have gone further.

But they constrained him, saying, Abide with us: for it is toward evening, and the day is far spent. And he went in to tarry with them.

And it came to pass, as he sat at meat with them, he took bread, and blessed *it*, and brake, and gave to them.

And their eyes were opened, and they knew him; and he vanished out of their sight.

And they said one to another, Did not our heart burn within us, while he talked with us by the way, and while he opened to us the scriptures?

Study

SELF-SUFFICIENCY *has never been God's plan for the life of His disciple.* Sometimes the trying, even *impossible* circumstances we face are not engineered by Satan (we give him far too much credit) but rather by God Himself! He wants His sons and daughters to trust Him so much that we will lean upon Him with all that we are, and believe that He knows what He is doing in our lives.

When we cast all of our cares upon God our Father and take up His yoke, we will indeed learn to lean upon Him and find rest for our souls. When Jesus invites us to come to Him, take His yoke, and learn of Him in Matthew 11:28-30, He is inviting you and me to become His disciples and thus learn to lean upon Him. Here we have God's Son giving all He had for us with such great compassion, love, and devotion to the Father and toward us. He did not boast of being equal with God, yet He submitted to Him. Meek does not mean weak. In fact, it is great strength. It is not proud or puffed up, arrogant or haughty. Meekness is humble, loving, and kind. Jesus Himself meekly leaned upon His Heavenly Father.

This yoke that Jesus offers us keeps us in step with Him and teaches us to lean upon Him in prayer. Sometimes we are tempted to lean toward our own feelings and understanding. When we come prayerfully to the Lord as a disciple, we have learned the true meaning of casting our cares upon Him as we take up His yoke. By being disciplined in taking up His yoke we no longer move in ourselves. Thus, we don't wear ourselves out by trying to move in our own strength and power or by using our own influence/popularity. God will allow us to go so far before He lovingly, sometimes firmly, pulls us back to Him so that He can complete His work in our lives. In this session, we will consider three people in Scripture as they prayerfully learned to lean and become yoked to Jesus' heart.

Learning to Lean on God and Not Our Own Scheme and Devices

First, let's consider Jacob. Rebekah, Jacob's mother, heard from the Lord.

> And the Lord said unto her, two nations are in thy womb, and two manner of people shall be separated from thy bowels; and the one people shall be stronger than the other people; and the elder shall serve the younger (Genesis 25:23).

Rebekah was told that she was carrying twins and that the youngest child would rule over the oldest. Jacob, being born second, already had the promise of the Lord that He would bless him. We see the story unfold as Jacob tried one scheme after another instead of leaning on the promises of God. How many times in our own lives do we try to work our own plans instead of prayerfully looking to God's promises? Like Jacob, we already have His promises, yet sometimes we will go ahead with our own plans instead of submitting to the Lord in prayer.

Jacob tricked his older brother out of his birthright, and then his father out of Esau's blessing. Esau was furious and *hated his brother*, which caused Jacob to fear for his own life so he ran to escape. Jacob got what he wanted, but it cost him his relationship with Esau. Jacob ran to his Uncle Laban's house (Genesis 27:41-45). On the way to his uncle's house, Jacob encountered the Lord in a dream. Jacob watched as angels went up and down a ladder, and the Lord spoke to him. The Lord promised to bless him and keep him and all of his seed.

> And Jacob awaked out of his sleep, and he said, Surely the Lord is in this place; and I knew it not. And he was afraid, and said, How dreadful is this place! this is none other but the house of God, and this is the gate of heaven (Genesis 28:16-17).

Can you even imagine? Instead of stopping there and submitting to the Lord, Jacob still had his own plan. The good thing Jacob did do was to make a vow to God that if he could return to his father's house in peace, the Lord would be his God. Although he was still working his own plan, Jacob recognized the voice of the Lord and anointed the rock there as Bethel, meaning *the house of the Lord*.

Maybe you have places in your own life, where you have heard from the Lord, and that place for you is the house of the Lord.

Maybe you anointed that place as your Bethel but then walked away. The Lord is calling you back to a place of prayer today.

Jacob continued his own way. When he came to his uncle Laban's house and saw Rachel, he fell in love with her and worked another one of his deals to have Rachel as his wife. This time Jacob schemed with another schemer and was tricked into marrying Rachel's older sister Leah. When Jacob realized he did not get what he wanted, he worked another deal with his uncle in order to win Rachel. Jacob continued to work deals with Laban, as his family was growing larger with children of his own.

There was strife between Jacob and his uncle, and Jacob started running again—this time to go back to his home. It occurred to him that he would have to pass by his brother Esau's house. Right away Jacob came up with a conniving plan in order to get to where he wanted to go. When Jacob learned that his brother was coming to him along with 400 men, he called out to God for protection. Instead of trusting God and leaning on Him, Jacob decided to flatter his brother, even calling him "lord," and tried to buy him off.

While preaching on this passage years ago, a pastor stated, "God will protect you but He will not pamper you." How true! God finally jerked Jacob up by his thigh (so to speak) when Jacob would not lean on the promises of God. Out of His love for Jacob and because of His promises, God wrestled with Jacob all through the night, until early the next morning (Genesis 32:24-30). He was positioning Jacob to realize that he needed to depend upon Him and cease all of his scheming. God even gave Jacob a new name, "Israel," that would change him from being the *deceiver* to a *prince*. Genesis 32:28 we read, "And he said unto him, thy name shall be called no more Jacob, but Israel for as a prince has thou power with God and with men, and hast prevailed." This name would reflect the new man Jacob would become—one who had learned to lean upon God, desire God's blessings, and trust Him with his heart.

The next morning after wrestling with God all night, Jacob (Israel) limped out to greet his brother. All schemes were gone, and Israel found forgiveness when met up with his brother Esau.

You will always find forgiveness when you lean upon the Lord. God has such great plans and love for us. He tells us,

> I know the thoughts that I think toward you, saith the Lord, thoughts of peace, and not of evil, to give you an expected end (Jeremiah 29:11, KJ21).

God knows how to divinely intervene in order to drive you to call upon Him in prayer and to seek Him with your whole heart. He will be there waiting to bless you.

> By faith Jacob, when he was dying, blessed both of
> the sons of Joseph; and worshipped, leaning upon
> the top of his staff (Hebrews 11:21).

Like Jacob, you might have tried things your own way and even devised your own plans and turned to others that were working their plans. These times may have left you spiritually and emotionally limping. But when you are willing to hold on until God blesses you and you learn to lean upon Him, you will have the peace and promises of the Lord in your life. God wants you to trust Him and to realize His promises in His Word for you. Learn prayerfully to lean upon Him so He can bless you and work His perfect plan for your life as His disciple.

Learning to Lean on God
When Your Supports are Removed

Let's look at David as an example. David was "a man after God's own heart" (Acts 13:22). He had everything going for him. He had the love of his wife Michal and of his best friend Jonathan. King Saul initially loved David and David had a close relationship with the king. The people all sang out praise to David because of all the great victories he had won in battle. Life was great for him. David was a good man, was greatly loved, and was enjoying great success. No doubt, like anyone would, he also enjoyed the praises of the people. Then little by little, all of these things that David had as his supports in life began to be taken away. Saul became jealous, and David had to flee for his life. He left behind all that he knew and loved and ended up emotionally alone.

When you lean upon your own props, things can and do change in life that will remove them from you, even when you are serving faithfully as David had been. 1 Samuel 21:10-15 shows that when the praises of the people start to turn against even someone as strong as David (who killed Goliath), it can change how you act. No longer is David portrayed as a mighty warrior or the son-in-law to the king. Now it is said that he appeared like a mad man and became afraid. David had gone to the King of Gath as he ran from Saul, and was leaning upon the favor of man. But he was disappointed and fear came into his heart.

The story doesn't end there. The Psalms are filled with examples of how David learned to lean upon God alone. In Psalm 34:1, David leaned upon the power of praising God as he stated, "I will bless the Lord at all times; His praise shall continually be in my mouth." When fear came knocking, David learned to lean upon the deliverance of the Lord from all of his fears (v. 4). The goodness of the Lord had become something David could "taste and see" (v. 8) as he leaned upon God for his substance. David was clothed in the righteousness of the Lord as he learned to lean upon the fear of the Lord alone. Finally, in the last part of Psalm 34 David learned to lean on his trust in the Lord. David found the Lord to be the redeemer of his soul (v. 22). Learning to lean upon the Lord in prayer is indeed the source of true joy for a disciple of Christ.

If you find yourself in a place where everyone and everything you had once depended upon for your happiness is no longer there, don't fret. God may just be positioning you to a place where you can learn to lean upon Him and find true joy as David did. When you learn to lean on God through trust and praise like David, you can join him in saying,

> For thou art great, and doest wondrous things: thou art God alone (Psalm 86:10).

Nothing says it better than the old hymn, "Leaning On the Everlasting Arms," written by Rev. E. A. Hoffman and A. J. Showalter. "What a fellowship, what a joy divine, leaning on the everlasting arms." It occurs to me, *why would anyone want to lean on any other arms? God's are the only everlasting arms that will take you safely and securely into eternal life with Him.*

Learning to Lean on God Even
When You Have to Pursue Him

These few examples are not an all-inclusive list of the different ways the Lord teaches us in Scripture to lean upon Him. With Jacob, we saw a man who had the promise of God for blessings, yet chose his own path, and with whom God wrestled until he learned to lean upon Him. The Divine Wrestler seemed that He wanted Jacob to let Him go. In reality, he desired for Jacob to pursue Him.

In David, we see a man after God's own heart who prospered in every way, and then one day found himself alone without all of those things upon which he had depended. God then caused David to realize that only through leaning upon Him and Him alone could he ever hope to find true happiness.

After Jesus' resurrection, on the Emmaus Road (Luke 24:13-32), the Bible said that Jesus while walking with the disciples "made as though" He would leave them. However, the disciples begged Him to stay with them. In truth, Jesus wanted the disciples to pursue Him! *When it seems the Lord is walking away from you, He wants you to pursue Him in prayer.*

There is another person that God has used in my own life to teach me to lean upon Him by pursuing Him. In Matthew 15:22-28 we find the woman from Canaan. We see the agony of this mother as she cried out "Have mercy on me!" *She pursued Jesus and found Him in His hiding place and worshipped Him!* When she pleaded with Jesus to deliver her daughter from the evil spirits, she was met with silence. It is an uncomfortable place to be—silence. Sometimes the Lord will discomfort you to get you to where He wants you to be.

Upon finally answering her, Jesus spoke of not giving the children's (Jews) bread to the dogs (Gentiles). This woman could have taken up the spirit of offense and walked away. She could have given up and left crying, frustrated, and hopeless.

How many times have you needed something from the Lord and not received the answer you were expecting? Did you continue to lean in to the Lord and prayerfully pursue Him like this precious mother did? She leaned in without losing her hope and trust in the Lord. She did not argue with Him and she still called Him "Lord." She seemed to know that all she needed were the crumbs from the table of the Lord Jesus when she responded with, "Truth, Lord: yet the dogs eat of the crumbs that fall from their masters' table," (Matthew 15:27). This is the response of faith Jesus wanted! This must have blessed Jesus as he commended her for her faith and spoke healing into her daughter's life from that very hour.

Just as the Lord brought healing to the woman's daughter, He is waiting for you to pursue Him so He can bless you! Wherever you find yourself in life right now, have you learned to lean upon Him? Are you depending upon others like David? Are you making your own plans and scheming to get what you want like Jacob? There is a way that brings true peace and happiness. When we learn to lean upon Him in intimate prayer, praying without ceasing, believing Him, giving thanks to Him, praising Him, doing spiritual warfare on our knees, and refusing to give up, we find true peace and happiness. That is when we have learned the power of prayer and we have learned to breathe, to live, and to having our being in Him! Only then can we be the disciples that He has called us to be as we intercede with God for others.

Praying, The *Breath* of Life

My Prayers to Pray

God, please give to me a burning desire to hear Your voice every day through the reading of Your Word and by the gentle guiding and prompting of the Holy Spirit.

Lord, please forgive me for my habit of making my own plans, devising my own strategies, and leaning to my own understanding of the situations and challenges of my life. I confess my fleshly habit of self-sufficiency.

Father, help me to live out Your Word every day which says, in Proverbs 3:5, 7, "Trust in the Lord with all thine heart; and lean not unto thine own understanding. Be not wise in thine own eyes: fear the Lord, and depart from evil."

Father God, help me to pray with faith and trust in You with peace in my heart because I know that You love me. If I acknowledge You in all the areas of my life, You will direct my paths.

Dear Lord, when I pray and do not sense Your presence and You do not seem to be answering my prayers, please send Your Holy Spirit to remind me that You have not truly turned from me. Instead, You are desiring for me to pursue You relentlessly with faith and love!

Questions for Discussion and Reflection

1. Do you really lean on the Lord, or do you sometimes lean on your own understanding of a situation?

2. Discuss the meaning of the statement, "self-sufficiency has never been God's plan for the life of His disciples." How has this statement been demonstrated in your own life?

3. In his earlier life, Jacob naturally took the road of self-sufficiency and scheming. As believers, do you feel we often plunge ahead with our own plans and strategies and then only later consult God about what His plan is?

4. Discuss Matthew 15:22-28 and the account of Jesus and the woman from Canaan. Was Jesus being rude to the woman? Or, was He wanting to draw her faith out into the open and cause her to lean on Him completely as she realized that He wanted to give her what she was asking of Him?

5. Have you ever sought God but felt as though He was running away from you or wouldn't take your call? Do you believe He ignored you because He didn't care or maybe He wanted to get your attention so that you would pursue Him in prayer?

6. When you think back over your life and the months or years you have followed Jesus, have there been key times in your life when (like Jacob) you wrestled with God in prayer? Do you feel that you continued to wrestle in prayer until God moved? How is Jacob's wrestling God like praying through?

7. What did you learn through your own struggles in life? Can you praise God for times of struggle and see how He was working in your life?

8. Are you going through something even now that God is wanting to use to teach you to trust Him, lean upon Him, and pursue Him? Have you depended upon props or have you realized that God is all you need?

SESSION SEVEN
My Prayer Journal

Praying, The *Breath* of Life

Praying
Is *Interceding* With God

DR. O. WAYNE BREWER

SESSION EIGHT

Scriptures

Exodus 17:9-13

And Moses said unto Joshua, Choose us out men, and go out, fight with Amalek: tomorrow I will stand on the top of the hill with the rod of God in mine hand.

So Joshua did as Moses had said to him, and fought with Amalek: and Moses, Aaron, and Hur went up to the top of the hill.

And it came to pass, when Moses held up his hand, that Israel prevailed: and when he let down his hand, Amalek prevailed.

But Moses hands were heavy; and they took a stone, and put it under him, and he sat thereon; and Aaron and Hur stayed up his hands, the one on the one side, and the other on the other side; and his hands were steady until the going down of the sun.

And Joshua discomfited Amalek and his people with the edge of the sword.

Isaiah 53:12

. . . And he bare the sin of many, and made intercession for the transgressors.

Ezekiel 3:16-17

And it came to pass at the end of seven days, that the word of the Lord came unto me, saying,

Son of man, I have made thee a watchman unto the house of Israel: therefore hear the word at my mouth, and give them warning from me.

Ezekiel 22:30

And I sought for a man among them, that should make up the hedge, and stand in the gap before me for the land, that I should not destroy it: but I found none.

Matthew 6:10

Thy kingdom come, Thy will be done in earth, as it is in heaven.

John 17:9

I pray for them: I pray not for the world, but for them which thou hast given me; for they are thine.

John 17:15

I pray not that thou shouldest take them out of the world, but that thou shouldest keep them from the evil.

John 17:20-21

Neither pray I for these alone, but for them also which shall believe on me through their word;

That they all may be one; as thou, Father, art in me, and I in thee, that they also may be one in us: that the world may believe that thou hast sent me.

Romans 8:26-27

Likewise the Spirit also helpeth our infirmities: for we know not what we should pray for as we ought: but the Spirit itself maketh intercession for us with groanings which cannot be uttered.

And he that searcheth the hearts knoweth what is the mind of the Spirit, because he maketh intercession for the saints according to the will of God.

Hebrews 7:24-25

But this man, because he continueth ever, hath an unchangeable priesthood.

Wherefore he is able also to save them to the uttermost that come unto God by him, seeing he ever liveth to make intercession for them.

Praying, The *Breath* of Life

SESSION EIGHT

Study

THERE I WAS IN WICHITA, KANSAS, sitting in the conference room of a church talking with the pastor about his staff. One particular name came up and I said, "I believe she is an intercessor." The pastor gave me a response that was quite profound. He said, "Yes, she wants what God wants." Powerful! That is the key to intercessory prayer. When I intercede, I don't want what I want, I want what God wants no matter what. Intercessory praying doesn't only intercede to God; it also intercedes with God to accomplish His perfect, wise will in any situation or with any person.

What Is Intercessory Prayer?

An intercessor or *prayer warrior*, as we used to call them when I was growing up, should know that he or she is a partner with God. A true intercessor is on God's team and understands Jesus' prayer,

> Thy kingdom come, Thy will be done in earth, as it is in heaven (Matthew 6:10).

When one intercedes in prayer, one makes a plea for something or someone else. Intercede comes from the

Latin word, *intercedere*. (*Inter* means *between* while *cedere* means *to go*.) Intercedere then, carries the meaning of *going between* or *standing in the gap*.

To Make Intercession

In speaking of Jesus Christ as our Heavenly High Priest, Hebrews 7:25 says that He "ever liveth to make intercession" for us. The phrase "make intercession," in Greek, is derived from the *entunchano*, (#1793), which in this passage means *to entreat* (in favor or against), or to *deal with or make intercession*. Intercession, therefore, carries the whole idea of going between two parties for the purpose of entreating. An intercessor is a living go-between, while the intercessor's ministry is a ministry of intercession. An intercessor mediates (with a view toward reconciliation) between two parties or two extremes.

No wonder that a prime directive from God to His church is found in 2 Corinthians 5:18, "And all things are of God, who hath reconciled us to himself by Jesus Christ, and hath given to us the ministry of reconciliation." As Christ reconciled us to God, so is the church to go out into the harvest of souls and evangelize them with a view toward reconciling them to God. The ministry of intercession is an essential element of fulfilling the Great Commission of Christ.

The ministry of intercession is pointed to in Ezekiel 22,

And I sought for a man among them, that should make up the hedge, and stand in the gap before me for the land, that I should not destroy it: but I found none (v. 30).

Ezekiel 22:30 not only emphasizes the go-between nature of an intercessor, but also shows that the ministry of intercession through the power of God can shape events! Indeed, in the very next verse, the Lord says that He poured out (His) indignation upon them precisely because there was no intercessor to be found. As Christ's church seeks to fulfill her Great Commission, the need for prayer intercessors in spiritual warfare is becoming abundantly clear around the world. The Holy Spirit is calling church congregations to breathe corporate prayerful intercession for the church, our nation, and the world!

Purposes of Intercessory Prayer

The purpose of intercessory prayer always has the ultimate goal of carrying out Jesus' model prayer that God's will be "done in earth as it is in heaven," (Matthew 6:10). For God's will to be done in the world naturally calls for spiritual warfare against the adversary and this corrupt world system. Intercessory prayer then, stands at the forefront of the spiritual artillery of the church as she lays siege to the strongholds of the kingdom of darkness.

Intercessory prayer is fervent prayer. Rather than a formal poetic prayer of phrasing, it is a passionate prayer of power. Intercession has the sense of travailing, much like a woman giving birth to new life. Paul uses the Greek term *Odino*, (#5605) when he says "My little children, of whom I travail in birth again until Christ be formed in you," (Galatians 4:19). *Odino* means, *to travail in birth*. *Odino*, like *mochthos* #3449, (*painfulness*) in 2 Corinthians 11:27, and *tikto*, #5088, (*travail*) or (*beget*) in John 16:21, has the idea of a painful process of travailing in order to give birth to something new. So then, interceding in prayer is both standing as a go-between and bringing something into being through travail. In praying for God's will to be done, there are numerous specific needs for which a believer can serve as a go-between and indeed, travail in intercessory prayer.

There are many intercessory go-between prayers in scripture that are recorded as coming from the mouths of God's saints.

Abraham interceded to God for the city of Sodom and thus for his nephew Lot in Genesis 18:23-32. His intercession postponed judgment on Sodom temporarily and served to save the life of Lot and his daughters. *Intercessors have shaped history.*

When Joshua was fighting against Amalek, so long as Moses interceded with his hands upraised to God, Joshua prevailed. But when Moses lowered his hands, Joshua began to suffer defeat. By the assistance of Aaron and Hur, Moses' hands were continuously held up until sundown and total victory was claimed (Exodus 17:9-

13). This is an example of God receiving intercession and clearly, decisively responding to it.

In Numbers 14:13-19, Moses interceded to God on behalf of a rebellious Hebrew nation, and caused God to withhold immediate judgment upon them.

In Joel 2:15-17, the scriptures speak of sanctifying a fast, calling a solemn assembly and letting the priests "weep between the porch and the altar" interceding for God to spare His people and have mercy. Other intercessory prayers are recorded in Nehemiah 1 and Daniel 9 for God to restore His people, to deliver others from danger (Acts 12:5; Romans 15:31), and to bless His people (Numbers 6:24-26).

It was intercessors who prayed for the power of the Holy Spirit to come (Acts 8:15-17; Ephesians 3:14-17), for someone to be healed (1 Kings 17:20-21; Acts 28:8), for those in authority to rule well (1 Chronicles 29:19; 1 Timothy 2:1-2), for Christian growth (Philippians 1:9-11; Colossians 1:10-11), for effective pastors (2 Timothy 1:3-7), for effective mission work (Matthew 9:38; Ephesians 6:19-20), for the salvation of souls (Romans 10:1), and even for people to praise God (Psalm 67:3-5). The list of intercessory prayers recorded in the Word of God could go on, but suffice it to say that anything the Bible reveals to us as God's holy will for His people can legitimately be the purpose and goal of intercessory prayer. Remember, the accomplishing of God's will is always a blow against Satan's kingdom.

Jesus is the Supreme Intercessor, and is our High Priest in Heaven. He is the foundation of all intercession.

Even during His earthly ministry, Jesus prayed for the vast multitudes whom He came to seek and to save (Luke 19:10). In heartfelt brokenness, He wept over Jerusalem (Luke 19:41). Jesus interceded for His own disciples, both individually (Simon Peter in Luke 22:32) and as a group (John 17:6-20). The last intercessory prayer that He prayed during His earthly ministry was for His enemies while He was hanging on a cross (Luke 23:34).

Now resurrected and glorified, Christ's present ministry as our heavenly High Priest is to intercede on our behalf before the very throne of God. Jesus declares victory over Satan for the saints in Romans.

> Who is he that condemneth? It is Christ that died, yea rather, that is risen again, who is even at the right hand of God, who also maketh intercession for us (Romans 8:34).

As high priest, Christ enters the holy place in heaven "to appear in the presence of God for us" according to Hebrews 9:24. As our High Priest and Intercessor, Jesus Christ, " . . . is also able to save them to the uttermost that come unto God by him, seeing that he ever liveth to make intercession for them" (Hebrews 7:25). Without the intercession of Christ and His grace, we would all undoubtedly fall away into the captivity of sin of which we were once slaves. No wonder John tells us,

> And if any man sin, we have an advocate with the Father, Jesus Christ the righteous (1 John 2:1).

As we breathe intercessory prayer for the will of God, Christ continually intercedes for us.

The Holy Spirit: Intercessor for Intercessors

The believer may at times feel overwhelmed with the fury of the spiritual warfare around him or her. But take comfort in the truth that while Christ intercedes for the believer in heaven, our Comforter, the Holy Spirit is interceding for and through us as we fight the good fight here on earth. The Holy Spirit is very much involved in intercession.

As human beings, we often find our own intercessory praying to be spiritually frail, incomplete, and adrift in the ignorance of not knowing what to pray for or even how to pray. This is where the Holy Spirit comes to our rescue. He is the living provision for our weakness.

> Likewise the Spirit also helpeth our infirmities; for we know not what we should pray for as we ought: but the Spirit itself maketh intercession for us with groanings which cannot be uttered. And he that searcheth the hearts knoweth what is the mind of the Spirit, because he maketh intercession for the

saints according to the will of God (Romans 8:26-27).

So the Holy Spirit intercedes through our human spirit "according to the will of God." In this sense, the Holy Spirit is our Divine Guide and Equipper in prayer. Prayer should be thought of by the Christian not as an activity we do merely in our natural strength, but as a work of the Holy Spirit through us as we allow Him to partner with us to accomplish the perfect will of God. Pentecostals and Charismatics understand that praying in tongues is from the Holy Spirit and enhances the believer's intimacy with Jesus Christ.

The Greek phrase en *pneumati*, or *in the Spirit* essentially means in the spiritual realm and with the help of the Holy Spirit. This is what Paul is referring to in 1 Corinthians 14:2, "For he that speaketh in an unknown tongue speaketh not unto men, but unto God: for no man understandeth him; howbeit in the spirit he speaketh mysteries." Likewise in 1 Corinthians 14:14, "for if I pray in an unknown tongue, my spirit prayeth . . .". The Holy Spirit edifies our spirit and successfully communicates our inner needs and feelings (that we cannot even voice in our own language) to God in such a way that facilitates our prayers lining up perfectly with His will. There is something about praying *in the Spirit*, by the power of the Holy Spirit, that refreshes, recharges, restores, and rebuilds what our ministry, the cares of life, and spiritual warfare can take out of us.

The believer accesses the power and energy of the Holy Spirit as he intercedes in the Holy Spirit. As the Holy Spirit speaks through the believer in tongues, that believer edifies himself. Jude 1:20 exhorts the intercessor, "But ye, beloved, building up yourselves on your most holy faith, praying in the Holy Ghost." As Christ intercedes for the child of God in heaven, so the Holy Spirit intercedes through the child of God on earth. As in all things, when Christ commissions the Christian to do something He always provides the power to do it.

Intercessory Prayer of the Early Church

Corporate intercessory prayer was the norm rather than the exception for the early church. The 120 believers had been together in one accord in the Upper Room on the Day of Pentecost. They were waiting and praying, when "they were all filled with the Holy Ghost, and began to speak with other tongues, as the Spirit gave them utterance" (Acts 2:4). The early church also interceded on behalf of individual believers, as they did when they prayed for Simon Peter's release from jail (Acts 12:5, 12) and for the success of the ministry of Barnabus and Paul (Acts 13:3). Take note of Epaphras, who labored fervently in prayer for the Jews (Colossians 4:12). James tells the church elders to pray for the sick (James 5:14), and for believers to pray for one another (James 5:16). The church of the New Testament prayed powerfully and spontaneously in the Holy Spirit. In preparing for spiritual warfare, Paul admonishes believers as he admonished the Ephesians then to pray always "with all prayer and supplication in the Spirit" (Ephesians 6:18). This is what makes spiritual warfare truly *spiritual* rather than feeble and fleshly.

Dynamics of Intercession

Although there are several Greek words for prayer used in the New Testament, the two words which probably carry the essence of intercessory prayer are *proseuchomai,* #4336, a compound word which means to *supplicate,* or make a wish toward God, and *parakaleo* #3870, meaning *to call near* by *imploration* or *beseeching.* So then, when a believer is interceding, he or she is calling God so that a desired wish may be beseeched of God. This implies a nearness, or relationship between the supplicant (the intercessor) and God. Thankfully, this relationship is well established and strong. Again, Jesus is our Divine model. Appendix Two on *Intercessory Prayer Warriors and Prayer Leaders* will be a very helpful resource for this session.

What Intercession Brings to the Intercessor

In His travailing prayer in the garden of Gethsemane, Jesus prayed "*Abba,* Father, all things are possible unto thee" (Mark 14:36). Abba, a term of warm, gentle endearment, is used not only by Jesus, but also by the Holy Spirit as He prays through us. It appears then, that a significant function accomplished when we intercede in the Spirit is forging a paternal relationship between us and our Heavenly Father, creating an even more intimate bond. Note the two other New Testament uses of Abba, Father. Romans 8:15 tells us, ". . . but ye have received the spirit of adoption, whereby we cry, Abba, Father." Galatians 4:6 says, "And because ye are sons, God hath sent forth the Spirit of his Son into your hearts, crying, Abba, Father."

Clearly, the Apostle Paul's teaching to the early church at Rome, as well as Galatia, was that the Holy Spirit not only glorifies the Son in our praying, but draws our spirits closer to our Heavenly Father. It appears that the ministry of intercession, beyond the good it does for the object of our prayer, also benefits the spiritual well being of we who are doing the praying!

Types of Intercession

First, there is general intercession. A person functioning as a general intercessor may be given a prayer list, and they pray through that list and any other prayer requests that come to their attention. In a manner of speaking, general intercession fills in the gaps left by more specific intercession.

Second, there is crisis intercession. Crisis intercessors don't pray through a list, they pray for known emergency situations or God-given, Holy Spirit-prompted assignments until such time as the emergency has passed, or the Holy Spirit releases them. The Holy Spirit often prompts crisis intercession; however, it can also take place in direct response to human mechanisms such as a prayer chain ministry.

Third, there is personal intercession. A personal intercessor receives an assignment (hopefully from God) to pray for a leader or leaders in the church. The leader may be a pastor but does not necessarily have to be a pastor, or even a clergy person. A personal intercessor often feels a direct calling from the Lord to uphold a particular church worker on a regular basis.

Fourth, there is warfare intercession. All intercession can be easily classified as spiritual warfare (advancing the Kingdom of God and pushing back the Devil's kingdom). However, some intercession is specifically militant and has the nature of both resisting the adversary and aggressively attacking his gates of power—whether they are spiritual strongholds at a larger scale or a spiritual attack at the personal level.

Intercessory Manifestations of the Human Spirit

When true spiritual intercession is taking place things happen in the invisible realm that are manifested in a tangible, human way. The whole point of intercession is to travail for someone or something in order that things will happen in accordance with God's will and mercy. Things also happen with the intercessor. There are responses of the intercessor's human spirit that are manifestations of both the fervency and success of the prayer taking place.

Weeping

One response, which most every intercessor will experience at one time or another, is weeping. While the lack of weeping in no way signifies that an intercession is not authentic or fruitful, it is a common manifestation of the human spirit in response to the travail of fervent, heartfelt prayer. Joel 2 provides a clear example of the weeping response of intercession going up to God for someone else.

> Let the priests, the ministers of the Lord, weep between the porch and the altar, and let them say, Spare thy people, O Lord, and give not thine heritage to reproach, that the heathen should rule over them: wherefore should they say among the people, Where is their God? Then will the Lord be jealous for his land, and pity his people (vv. 17-18).

In the New Testament, weeping is exhorted for believers to do in compassionate empathy (and no doubt, intercession) for other believers. Romans 12:15 tells us to "weep with them that weep." Often weeping signifies the breaking and softening of the human heart as it becomes lost in the work of intercession and is made to conform itself to the heart of God.

Laughing

Laughing in the Spirit is a genuine intercessory response of the human spirit in the material world to the successful breakthrough of intercession in the spiritual world. It is a sign that God's will has been carried out.

He who sits in the heavens shall laugh; the Lord shall hold them in derision (Psalm 2:4).

I have experienced this phenomenon while in prayer for the physical healing of our daughter (we later saw the proof of that answered prayer.) As a pastor, I experienced laughing in the Spirit during an intense intercessory session just prior to planned revival services. The answer was released in the heavenlies! A week later the answer was seen in the evidence of an overwhelmingly powerful revival in which numerous people were saved, sanctified, baptized in the Holy Spirit, healed, and delivered.

Laughing and weeping can be part of every Pentecostal Christian's spiritual prayer life. For the intercessor, they are spiritually charged responses of the human spirit to unseen dynamics in the invisible realm.

Guidelines for Church-Based Intercessors

Pastors Need Intercessors

As we observed in our fifth session, Satan is at war with the church and thus devises plans of attack to hinder the growth and health of the Body of Christ. Paul speaks of the devices of the Devil in 2 Corinthians 2:11. In order to keep Satan from getting an advantage over us, believers "are not to be ignorant of his devices." This term device in this verse is *noema*, (#3540) meaning *perception* or *purpose*. Intercessory prayer is needed not only to bring about God's will in every situation, "Thy kingdom come, Thy will be done..." (Matthew 6:10), but also to counterattack Satan's thought out devices.

One device used effectively and destructively against the church in recent years is the devilish strategy of attacking pastors. These attacks render pastors weak through physical/mental burnout or may destroy their influence through moral failure, thereby scattering the local church flock and discrediting the work of the Lord. More than ever, pastors need personal intercessors. They are a strategic target of spiritual attack because they have higher visibility and influence in the local body. Higher levels of responsibility in God's church often attract higher levels of devils (demons to be precise), or at least a more intense, persistent attack. Why? Satan is a strategically minded foe. They need intercession to protect, guide, and strengthen them as they intercede, lead, and feed their flock of believers. Pastors, as well as every other Christian, need a prayer covering.

Intercessors Must be Properly Connected to the Church

It is essential that you realize that intercession is not above any other ministry in the congregation, or somehow independent of the spiritual leadership that resides in the office of pastor. If an intercessor is part of a prayer meeting, he or she needs to inquire whether or not the pastor and church sanction the meeting or if indeed the pastor even knows about it! It is unfortunate but true that some individuals begin a prayer meeting that becomes a gossip session dominated by either a critical spirit, an attitude of spiritual elitism, or both. This atmosphere reveals that such a group is not in the genuine unity of the Holy Spirit. If a prayer circle displays strife and dissension while sowing discord and character assassination, such a group needs to be disbanded and repentance forthcoming from those participants.

Intercessors involved in a group should maintain an attitude of love and be circumspect in sharing every prayer request or need mentioned within the meeting to the whole church. Prayer for protection of each other, as intercessors, should be offered for every participant. Intercessors should also be teachable and connect with the vision of the pastor. Remember that *intercessory prayer is not an end in itself*, but has the assignment of supporting and undergirding the mission and purpose statement of the church. This is to say that the intercessory prayer group is not a church within a church but is a loyal, servant-minded arm. Intercessors must be properly connected to the church. (For more information on group intercession within a church, see Appendix 2).

Talk to God, Not People

If a Christian is serving as an intercessor for any church leader or ministry, self-discipline of the tongue and spiritual wisdom must be two elements that are always part of their spiritual arsenal. There are pitfalls to be guarded against if you are to be used by the Holy Spirit as a personal intercessor to a pastor or other church leader. If God has called you to this ministry, He will sometimes reveal sins, problems, and specific circumstances to you that are unknown to other members of the church. You may even become a recipient of dreams and visions which give knowledge of events before they take place. This information is given to you to pray about, not to talk about. Do your talking to God, not to others.

Keep Pride at a Distance

Revelation from God can often accompany genuine, Spirit-led intercession. Be careful to avoid having pride over possessing information that only God can provide. You are to be a steward of this information and seek the face of God, asking Him to reveal to you whether or not you are to share it with the pastor or leader for whom you are praying. He or she may already be aware of the situation or fact and may simply need confirmation. Be humble and maintain a servant attitude. God called you to support the leader, not dictate terms to him or her. Never succumb to the satanic temptation to pervert your gift.

Armor-Bearer, Not Controller

As your pastor goes into spiritual warfare each week, he or she is involved in a struggle that requires the use of spiritual armor. It is the responsibility of the personal intercessors of the congregation (as it truly is for all of the members), to be spiritual armor-bearers for the pastor. A spirit of control or manipulation must be resisted as the satanic trap that it is. As a God-called intercessor, you are to help your leader. You are not to attempt to control your leader. In other words, keep self out of the spiritual equation. Seeking to control others is tantamount to witchcraft. As the Holy Spirit has no part of this behavior, you should constantly guard against falling into this trap of Satan.

The Lord has ordained leaders to serve His church, and your calling is to stand in the gap for them and pray for their protection, guidance, and anointing. If you feel the Holy Spirit is leading you to deliver a word of wisdom, knowledge, or prophecy to the leader, obey the Lord! If you feel divinely constrained to confront the leader about a sin, a problem, or another deviation from God's will, do so privately and share the message only with the individuals for whom it is intended.

Keep Spiritually Pure Motives

Never profane what the Holy Spirit tells you by sharing it inappropriately. Always evaluate your motives. Ask yourself, "Am I driven by pride, a desire to brag, or an emotional need to be closer to the pastor than other church members?" If so, God has not called you to be a personal intercessor. On the other hand, if you are interceding for a leader as a holy service—as unto the Lord—and you feel compelled to do so, then you should be faithful in your intercession. Remember the plea of Paul in Romans 15:

> Now I beseech you, brethren, for the Lord Jesus Christ's sake, and for the love of the Spirit, that ye strive together with me in your prayers to God for me (v. 30).

As Christ's present ministry is intercession, we, as His body, are called to intercede prayerfully for a lost, dying world. And why not? Praying truly is our *breath of life*.

Praying, The *Breath* of Life

My Prayers to Pray

O Lord, I know that as a disciple of Christ, Your battle is my battle and Your heart should be my heart. Help my will to crumble and be merged as one with Yours.

Heavenly Father, as a believer who is called to intercede for Your will, I repent of the gross sins of my nation and of the lukewarmness of the church. I ask You to forgive us and restore us so that we might be all You intended.

Lord, touch my heart and affections and help me to want what You want and be hurt over what hurts You. Help me to love everyone You love and pray in accordance with Your will.

Lord, as an intercessor, help me to be like an Aaron or Hur to my pastor and never someone who seeks to usurp his/her God-given leadership.

My Father that is in heaven, I pray Thy Kingdom come and Thy will be done in me, my family, my church, and in my nation, just as Your will is done in heaven. Please use me to be a faithful intercessor.

Praying, The *Breath* of Life

Questions for Discussion and Reflection

1. In considering Ezekiel 22:30 (where the Lord seeks for someone to stand in the gap), am I responding to His search for an intercessor, or have I been satisfied to allow my pastor to carry the full burden of our congregation on his back? Am I AWOL or have I truly joined the Lord's army of prayer warriors?

2. In Exodus 17:9-13, who won the battle against the Amalekites; Joshua (the soldier), Moses (the leader), or Aaron and Hur? What significance can intercessors today draw from the example of Aaron and Hur?

3. How does the Holy Spirit help us to pray? Is He an intercessor as well? What is the significance of Romans 8:26-27?

4. In praying intercessory prayers to God, am I truly praying in accordance with His divine will? Or are my objectives self-centered or according to my own understanding? Am I confident that my intercessory prayer is God centered?

5. As I intercede, are my motives right? Is my praying properly aligned with what God's Word teaches?

SESSION EIGHT

My Prayer Journal

Praying, The *Breath* of Life

Praying
The *Breath* of life

Praying, The *Breath* of Life

APPENDIX ONE

Praise Takes Different Forms

(Excerpt used with permission from *Fighting the Good Fight* (p. 73, 74 & 75), by Dr. O. Wayne Brewer)

Praise Takes Different Forms

Genuine praise and worship to God manifests itself in different forms. Examples of praise are many and varied throughout Scripture. Here are a few examples:

Wave Offering, Leviticus 8:27

Clapping, Psalm 47:1

Dancing, 2 Samuel 6:14

Singing, Psalm 47:6

Lifting of Hands, Nehemiah 8:6

Laughter, Psalm 126:2

Exclaiming "Amen," Nehemiah 8:6

Crying Aloud, Isaiah 12:6

Bowing the Head, Nehemiah 8:6

Leaping, Luke 6:23

Shouting, Psalm 35:27

Speaking in Tongues, Acts 10:46

Our praise unto the Lord is a dual-purpose action.

First it glorifies God and exalts His Name as it makes our own hearts glad. Second, praise serves as a spiritual dynamic which strengthens our heart even as it positively changes our circumstances from a situation of frailty and sadness into a situation of strength and gladness.

Praise is the "shout of the Lord in the camp" that terrorizes our spiritual enemy. It is a weapon that can be used even while you are using another weapon in combat. Praise nourishes the joy of the Lord "which is your strength."

APPENDIX TWO

An Effective Prayer Warrior and an Effective Prayer Leader

(Used by permission from *Corporate Intercession: Empowering the Local Church* with special thanks to Josie Cavazos and Jubilee On the Ridge, Pastors Steve and Sandy Grandy)

<u>Description of an Effective Prayer Warrior</u>

1. One who believes that prayer works and will not be moved from that principle of God

2. One who has no private agenda, only wants to pray

3. One who loves to pray and sees all solutions coming from prayer first

4. One who is faithful to stand in the gap instead of pointing to the gap

5. One who has compassion for the lost and is willing to pray at any time for anyone

6. One who makes praying a priority and will be faithful to come to corporate intercession

7. One who has a heart for the pastoral staff and other leaders

8. One who likes to be in the background in their prayer closet and does not need attention for their work

9. One who understands authority and knows the importance of being under authority

10. One who knows and believes in the power of unity and one accord

11. One who does not get offended and does not give offenses

12. One who does not have a critical spirit

<u>Description of an Effective Prayer Leader</u>

A pastor should not only be a leader and example to the flock under his care, in the area of intercessory prayer himself, but he must encourage individual and corporate prayer in the congregation. He should also truly know those whom he would appoint as prayer leaders. Following is a description of an effective prayer leader.

1. One who has paid the price to be faithful in the above twelve areas

2. One who is submitted to the pastor's vision for the church and the prayer group and supports and defends that vision

3. One who does not seek a position but accepts it out of obedience to God and his pastor

4. One who has a strong prayer life

5. One who hears from God about the needs of the pastor even before the pastor asks for prayer, and is always there to support the pastor

6. One who can keep the secrets God has given to him/her about the prayer needs of His anointed men and

women; one whom the pastor and leaders can trust not to spread confidential matters all over the church

7. One who communicates closely with the pastor and other leaders and goes to prayer when there is a difference of opinion, praying for God's will to prosper, regardless of who is right

8. One who does not have a need to control and does not have to have his own way

9. One who is humble, teachable, and flexible himself and continues to challenge the intercessors to grow

10. One who is whole emotionally. One who does not bring his emotions to prayer, such as bitterness, anger, hurts, or gossip

11. One who is able to correct in love and will correct and not display harshness

12. One who tithes. This is the test of those who are truly committed to building the vision of the body through the pastor

Praying, The *Breath* of Life

APPENDIX THREE

Prayer Beyond the Church Walls

1. Prayer for Those Outside the Church Walls

   The intercessory warfare of the local congregation
   must always have as one of its foremost priorities, the
   influencing, reaching, and winning of the lost. Prayer
   must reach beyond the church walls of praise and
   worship to God. Although worship is unquestionably
   primary to the purpose of the congregation; winning
   the lost is also a form of practical worship to God.
   Organized corporate prayer that specifically targets
   those people *outside the Church walls* who never hear
   a sermon, never attend a Bible study, and are never
   confronted with the Good News of Christ should be
   an ongoing offensive prayer war against the enemy.

   Maps of the community should be prayed over as well
   as individual streets. When pastoring, I made sure
   that we specifically prayed over three selected streets
   every week. These *prayer streets of the week* were
   listed in the church bulletin (an alphabetical listing
   taken from a city map) and brought before God
   during corporate intercession night. The intercession

that went up to God was that every individual who lived, worked or attended school on that street would somehow have a revelation of Jesus Christ either through a Christian friend, stranger, or perhaps by hearing of Jesus on the radio or television. We even saw visitors attend our church on the very Sunday or that same week that we spotlighted and prayed for their street (thus praying for them)!

2. Prayer Walks

The practical idea behind *prayerwalking* is to spiritually *soften up* the same area in which you intend to harvest souls. While some may be skeptical, God does still answer prayers prayed in accordance with His desire to save souls. When a congregation is engaged in prayerwalking, streets and neighborhoods are assigned to church members (according to where they live), for the purpose of walking through areas and praying for the residents of every dwelling to become open to the Gospel (or strengthened in the Lord if they are already believers). Often a doorknob hanger is left on each door that says:

> *Hello, we just want you to know that a member of New Life Church of God is your neighbor. They have prayed for God's best for you and your family. If you wish to have a personal need brought to God in prayer (and kept confidential) you may call 555-432-1000*

at the New Life prayer center. Thank you!
Signed _____, your
neighbor.

Prayer-walking is a practical way of preparing an area for visitation and virtually anyone in the congregation can do it. It is not intended as a substitute for evangelism but rather as a *pre-evangelism* outreach. In prayer-walking the spiritual and the tangible are combined through body ministry to take a community for Christ. It is time to take the presence and prayers of a concerned, compassionate Church to the streets of our communities.

Praying, The *Breath* of Life

APPENDIX FOUR

1. Fasting is a primary means of restoration. By humbling us, fasting releases the Holy Spirit to do His revival work within us. This takes us deeper into the Christ life and gives us a greater awareness of God's reality and presence in our lives.

2. Fasting reduces the power of self so that the Holy Spirit can do a more intense work within us.

3. Fasting helps to purify us spiritually.

4. Fasting increases our spiritual reception by quieting our minds and emotions.

5. Fasting brings a yieldedness, even a holy brokenness, resulting in an inner calm and self-control.

6. Fasting renews spiritual vision.

7. Fasting inspires determination to follow God's revealed plan for your life.

Praying, The *Breath* of Life

APPENDIX FIVE

Five Biblical Elements of Corporate Prayer

(Used by permission and with special thanks to Jon Graff who lectured on this topic on August 23, 2013).

There is something powerful and dynamic that happens when more believers are involved together in prayer. God does great things . . .

1. *When you pray corporately and recognize that God is your only solution.* Ezra 8:21-23 demonstrates corporate prayer and total reliance upon God. Too often we seek God's will with our mind instead of His Holy Spirit in our heart.

2. *When you pray corporately and narrow the focus of your praying.* In Acts 12:5, Peter was in prison, but the church corporately prayed with the one focus of freeing Peter from imprisonment.

3. *When you pray corporately with one voice.* Again, in both Ezra 8:21-23 and in Acts 12:5, the people prayed with "one voice."

4. *When you pray corporately and invoke the presence of God.* In 2 Chronicles 6 and 7 Solomon invoked the presence of God and God responded with the mighty coming in of His presence.

5. *When you pray corporately in one accord.* In Acts 1:14; 2:1, these believers had been and continued (on the Day of Pentecost) to be in one accord (of one mind and heart).

APPENDIX SIX

The Names of God

Praise and worship the Name of God.
Confess and declare His Name over your life and the
lives of those you love!

Jehovah	I Am	Exodus 3:14
Jehovah-Rohi	I Am-My Shepherd	Psalm 23:1
Jehovah-Tsidkenu	I Am-Our Righteousness	Jeremiah 33:16
Jehovah-Shammah	I Am-Is There	Ezekiel 48:35
Jehovah-Sabaoth	I Am-Lord Of Hosts	Isaiah 51:15
Jehovah-M'kaddesh	I Am-Who Sanctifies	Leviticus 20:8
Jehovah-Nissi	I Am-My Banner	Exodus 17:15
Jehovah-Shalom	I Am-Is Peace	Judges 6:23-24
Jehovah-Rophe	I Am-He Heals	Exodus 15:26
Jehovah-Jireh	I Am-He Provides	Genesis 22:14
Jehovah Gmolah	I Am-The God of Recompense	Jeremiah 51:6

Confess and declare His Name over
the church you attend!

ABOUT THE AUTHORS

Dr. O. Wayne and Pamela R. Brewer

Dr. O. Wayne and Rev. Pamela R. Brewer, ordained ministers with the Church of God, have spent their lives answering the disciples' request to "teach us to pray." In their roles as pastors, state bishops, and conference speakers, they have preached, taught, and trained countless believers to embrace fervent, biblical praying as the central activity of Christian discipleship. Wayne and Pam love to serve and build up God's people.

Made in the USA
Columbia, SC
07 September 2023

22597566R00161